HOW INDUSTRIAL ADVERTISING AND PROMOTION CAN INCREASE MARKETING POWER

W. H. GROSSE

amacom

A DIVISION OF
AMERICAN
MANAGEMENT
ASSOCIATION

© 1973 AMACOM
A division of American Management Association, Inc., New York.
All rights reserved. Printed in the United States of America.

This publication may not be reproduced, stored in a retrieval system,
or transmitted in whole or in part, in any form or by any means,
electronic, mechanical, photocopying, recording, or otherwise,
without the prior written permission of the Association.

International standard book number: 0-8144-5307-4
Library of Congress catalog card number: 72-82872
First printing

PREFACE

There were several motivations for writing this book. The most proximate a special annual issue of an excellent trade magazine for industrial design engineers. This was a splendid piece of editorial work, providing valuable information for its highly specialized audience. Editorially it was magnificent. The content virtually guaranteed intense interest, high readership, and repeated reference. It reached a most potent spectrum of individuals—the engineers responsible for the innovation, quality, and performance of industrial products. The readers were the highly trained men who, year by year, design new industrial machinery, more efficient industrial processes, and improved industrial materials. From these fountainheads flow the steady streams of new and better products, improved methods of manufacture, and more efficient processes. To this special issue, like bees to an old-fashioned cider press, flew a swarm of advertisers. The periodical was fat. However, a systematic reading of the advertisements—cover to cover—had this writer alternating between admiration and acute stomach cramps. Between the covers of this *objet d'art* could be found all the mild, chronic, and acute diseases that afflict industrial promotion. If it in-

v

cluded the good, vigorous, and sound, it also included the feeble, confused, misdirected, and bad. Side by side nestled horrible examples of how to miss the boat and marvelous examples of how to hit the bull's-eye.

Judged purely on the basis of graphic arts, the eye appeal of practically all the ads in this issue was excellent. The sickness of so many, the cause of so much money being wasted lay within. Indeed the same syndrome can be found in any trade magazine—but not in such bulk.

My reaction was immediate and profound. I decided that setting down some basic principles would help the industrial-product marketers recognize the potency of the marketing tool we can capsulize as IA&SP—industrial advertising and sales promotion. These principles must stress the proper construction, sharpening, and employment of the tool. They should frankly describe its essential nature. They should face up to both its strengths and weaknesses. Fortunately, while the art is long, the basic guidelines are commendably concise. They could well assist industrial marketers and their agencies to direct their efforts and invest their money more wisely. Certainly if this book is ever read by concerned specialists in Germany, France, Italy, and the Benelux countries it can make a significant contribution. Because if a sizable portion of the industrial promotion effort of U.S. companies can be judged ill-conceived, unsoundly based, and flapping in the wind, the same maladies are epidemic in Europe—as an examination of the Continent's trade magazines will show.

This harsh judgment is not leveled at the appearance (or at the surface creativity) of certain advertisements in the special annual issue. With a few exceptions, their appearance was superb. Rather it is directed at their weak marketing base, at their creaky foundations, at the obvious fact that too many had no marketing plan underpinning at all. Since media advertising is only the visible tip of the industrial promotion iceberg, my reaction to this mammoth special issue was my first motivation.

My second was prompted by more than 20 years of watching capable industrial advertising managers get ulcers because their potential contribution to marketing progess has been largely ignored, badly used, misdirected, or relegated to the position of being the most expendable ingredient in the marketing mix.

Yet another prompting factor has been the experience of witnessing the grim spectacle of a number of competent advertising agencies trying to deal with the hydra-headed problem of creating advertising programs for industrial accounts. The billings are relatively minuscule. The products, to the uninitiated, appear sickeningly dull. The technical product benefits, with the best will in the world, seem esoteric, labyrinthine, and "unreal." The creative scope appears dull, limited, and beset with technical pitfalls. The buying influences are diffuse. The buying motivations mired in technicalese are unbelievable, and most often they are unknown or incomprehensible. The information on the market provided to the agency is usually vague and sketchy, often inaccurate and incomplete, sometimes nonexistent.

Finally, I was moved by the recurring confessions of bafflement from trade magazine publishers and media representatives. There are almost 2,000 of these periodicals, and they cover every conceivable trade. This group has a most intimate and detailed knowledge of specialized industries. Often their knowledge of markets, industrial needs, and buying factors is better than the information possessed by the marketers. An experienced trade-media representative will know of crying needs in the trade his publication serves. In contacting manufacturers, he sees again and again products or services that superbly meet these needs. But the producers do not advertise at all or they advertise wrongly. The media representative's plight is the saddest of all. The agency's media department, its account man, and the client's advertising department all stand between him and what is most frequently at the heart of the problem: the manufacturer's marketing or sales department.

In summation, IA&SP lies in a dim penumbra, subsisting wanly on the edge of the sunlit fields of massive consumer-product advertising and promotion. Consumer-product marketers are acutely aware of the essential value of advertising and promotion in their marketing mix; industrial marketers, rarely. Except for a few astute and specialized firms, advertising agencies view strictly industrial accounts with a massive lack of enthusiasm; they are carried with staunch fortitude as low-profit poor relations who have to be cared for. As for ambitious young people making a career of advertising, an industrial promotion job is too often the one they take until they can get into the "big time" with a packaged-goods company or an agency that handles glamorous consumer-product accounts. Can the challenge of promoting an ultrasonic welding tool possibly match that of flaky, bake-&-serve croissants, a transatlantic passenger service, or perfumed facial tissues?

Unfortunately the focus—all down the line—is distorted. By precedent. By attitude. By organization. By method. By the absence of a common base of understanding. And by different mixtures of these—in companies and their agencies, and among individuals.

Advertising and promotion can be a vital, potent
force in industrial marketing . . . when solidly
based, ably conceived, properly employed.

As a career, industrial advertising and sales promotion can be vastly satisfying. Frequently, industrial promotion achievements are far more spectacular in their results than the most sophisticated and extensive consumer-product programs. As a profit source for an agency, the same can apply. If agencies will risk an initial investment of time and effort to build significant programs—solidly based, rationally directed, and creatively viable—for industrial products, they need not be restricted to the media discount for compensation. The compensation an agency can receive from industrial accounts can be most attractive and far more stable. A satisfied industrial-product manufacturer will be found quite amenable to paying a supplementary service fee for results. But they must be *tangible* results—in measurably larger sales and marketing success, not results in the form of catchy-clever creative approaches, spectacular impact, high readership scores, or extensive ancillary merchandising. The industrial account will pay willingly and well for sound, integrated programs built to help solve the marketing problem and to assist with the selling task—regardless of the seemingly plebeian nature of the tools provided. And this is the task of promotion—to help make the marketing machine run more smoothly and perform more effectively.

Hence, this pragmatic volume can make a significant contribution, if for no other reason than because it attempts to bring the disparate segments of the overall industrial marketing and promotion task—as a discipline—into synergistic harmony. Its purpose is to sharpen focus. It does this by dogmatically stating some bald and basic principles, by outlining a method of approach that is basic—perhaps even primitive—but rational, by detailing some workable formulas by which effective advertising and sales promotion tools can be created, and by segmenting the overall marketing and promotion task so that the responsibility for each contributing part is vested in the logical function. And it does so, further, by bluntly telling each segment of the marketing team what contribution must come from each to make the promotion component an effective contributor to the marketing job. The following pages will show that the marketing mix can better nourish profitability when fortified with adequate, rational, and effective promotion. Unfortunately, advertising and promotion is in large measure the most often misunderstood, misused, and neglected ingredient.

In summary, this book attempts to orient the discipline of IA&SP in the marketing function, provide a practical approach to its employment, to suggest some pragmatic approaches to "how to do it." It offers guidelines, establishes benchmarks, and points out potential pitfalls.

Nowhere in these pages will you find examples of what I consider a good or bad advertisement. You will, however, find fundamental principles whose observance or violation will make industrial advertisements or promotion campaigns either effective or impotent. You will find only the barest commentary on what we can term the surface creativity of advertisements;

nothing on the relative effectiveness of various publications. And I am acutely aware that detailed specialist techniques for creating the various kinds of promotion tools are amply covered in a variety of excellent publications.

What you will find is an ordered, logical approach to the creation and operation of industrial promotion as a potentially powerful instrument of marketing. If this work does no more than clear the deck and adjust the compass for the discipline's most effective employment, it will give both marketing management and independent practitioners a solid base on which to build.

W. H. Grosse

CONTENTS

INDUSTRIAL ADVERTISING AND SALES PROMOTION: Its Vision of Itself

We are first going to examine a *function* within a business. The type of business is one that makes technical products that are sold to other industrial businesses. Our analysis and thesis will be confined to developing concepts so fundamental they may be applied by the small as well as the large corporation. We will develop principles that can optimize the effectiveness of modest, low-cost programs as well as the most elaborate undertakings. They may be applied by a "department," a single industrial advertising and sales promotion (IA&SP) practitioner, or by outside agencies that supply the promotion service. The neophyte in industrial advertising may find them revelatory; the sophisticate may find them primitive and self-evident. But no matter. The Ten Commandments have yet to be surpassed as a basic codification of morality—and few codes have been more ignored in whole or in part.

The starting point must be the vision that the practitioner has of his discipline, its function, and his relation to it.

In any discussion that attempts to establish a unity out of a dichotomy, to create a system amid confusions, to overcome specious reasoning with logic, a definition of terms is vital. All concerned must be talking of the same thing, or the result is the Mad Hatter's tea party. To make clear what IA&SP's vision of itself is—or should be—it is essential to reach a common semantic ground. We have already defined the kind of business endeavor; now it is necessary to agree on the nature of the function.

The function of IA&SP is to create all the tools of marketing, devise the integrated programs that employ them, and execute the programs in the field—for the purpose of most efficiently and effectively selling the product.

The "function" may be provided to the manufacturer or marketer as a service by an advertising agency, by an internal advertising and promotional manager working with outside services, or by a department head with a "department" segmented by product assignment or special expertise.

This definition sets the parameters. It delimits the function's vision of itself, orients it in the marketing operation, sets the scope of its responsibilities, and identifies its proper organizational niche in the company. Unless IA&SP's function is understood and accepted by top management and marketing or sales management, its effectiveness and operating efficiency will be hobbled. The function is integral; no parts of its responsibility spectrum can be separated out and vested piecemeal in other functions of the business. It is a discipline distinct from the public relations function and from the industrial and employee relations functions. It should not be overloaded with ancillary responsibility, mismated, or cannibalized. Most pertinently—no part of it should be sent to dwell in an ivory tower with "Advertising" emblazoned over its sacred portal.

This hard-and-fast definition is binding on the range of the function's responsibilities and its placement in the organization. It extends to every step—from creation to execution—in applying the tools of its trade to the job of selling. The function should report to the executive echelon responsible for marketing—at whatever level is most directly accountable for establishing, maintaining, or increasing sales volume. The function is most efficient when all its parts—planning, creating, production, and execution—are centered in a single individual or department head. Its performance is most effective when it is integrated with marketing, when its output is judged by the sales executive most directly concerned with sales results. Administratively, the function may be discharged as a staff service or established as a line operation. It is a matter of choice for the particular organization. There are virtues and vices in both.

As suggested in Exhibit 1, the most logical choice of line or staff is generally dictated by the size and complexity of the business. Whichever way, the principle of integrating the service with and establishing its accountability directly to line marketing management is vitally important. When it is transgressed, the resulting ills can be legion.

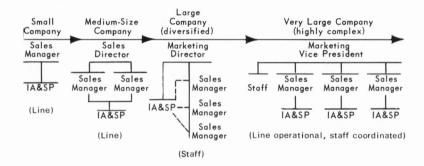

Exhibit 1. Positioning in the organization.

IA&SP is an instrument of marketing. The individual responsible for it is part of the marketing team. The function is an essential component of marketing planning. The discipline contributes its special expertise to the marketing program. It carries out its own assigned task as part of the sales program—just as do the technical service team; the order, shipping, and billing organization; the sales force in the field. Its financial support comes from the same source that accepts all other selling expenses. Thus, both its reason for being and accountability for performance rest with the marketing department.

With this as its basis, what vision must IA&SP take of itself? Since T. Levitt's article "Marketing Myopia" appeared over a decade ago in the *Harvard Business Review,* corporations, departments, and individuals have made a fetish of self-appraisal. This looking inward— realistically and objectively—frequently turns up some astonishing revelations. We are in populous and distinguished company when we take a hard look inward at IA&SP. It can be especially salutary if the discipline is one we make our life work or the function one that we offer for sale as a service. As with appraising a corporation or product, we return to fundamentals and break out of the habit cage. The company's view of the IA&SP function can be distorted by many factors, including tradition, organization, precedent, personnel limitations, favoritism for a particular kind of sales expertise, and blinkered vision.

To set the parameters of the IA&SP function, we can make two broad strokes. First, the function should contribute input to every action that affects the selling effort; second, it should assume complete responsibility for everything that requires "communication." These two strokes encompass a great deal, but as with trigonometry, there is a definite beginning and a distinct end.

The beginning is marked by the conception of trademarks and the graphic appearance of packages; the end is reached at the point of routine call-backs on established customers. Between these two poles, the IA&SP function is the planner, creator, and executor of the seven categories of selling tools and the programs that put them to use. Both the "tools" and "programs" will be taken up later. At this point, we can set its scope as embracing, permeating, and contributing to all the facets of selling. It is the salesman for the product in every manifestation and form distinct from the living body in the neat business suit who hands a calling card to a prospective buyer. It is the image creator for the product or company in every form from the sign on the roof and the design of the trademark to the order acknowledgment; it is the communicator of the existence and benefits of the product in every form from the catalog to its advertising, printed matter, and audio-visual presentations. It is the "packager" of the market strategy's "selling proposition." It is the creator and dispatcher of all "mechanical" selling devices charged with begetting a particular kind of action. It is the maker of weapons for the marketing armory.

In the mind's eye, one can see well-founded industrial advertising managers (happily free of the primitive problems) lift their eyebrows. "Okay," the voices say, "the IA&SP function is responsible to marketing for all the tools of selling. Why pick it to so many pieces?"

There are several reasons. Even in the most sophisticated companies this recognition often does not exist. In small and large companies, the function is blurred or diluted or both. And most important, with responsibility must go authority.

The range spread of responsibility means *a priori* that the IA&SP function must be given proper governance over these various levels of action. The function's charter in the company should stipulate the authority to provide input, carry out action, and be the final decision maker on all the contributing components of marketing communications. And the function's personnel capability must be equal to the task.

The highest degree of effectiveness and coordination is attained when the responsibility and authority are centered in a single individual and this individual's own line of responsibility extends upward to a single marketing executive. Unless this charter and direct line of authority is established, effective IA&SP, even with goodwill and the best intentions, will be unlikely to result; integration of promotion and marketing effort will be difficult if not impossible; and coordination for maximum effectiveness will be lost. There may then evolve the chaos of field salesmen governing creative approaches, technologists creating jawbreaking trademarks, production managers designing packages, technical service men producing sales literature, sales managers selecting media, and everyone writing and illustrating the advertisements.

The opposite side of the responsibility coin is the function's obligations. There are two:

INNOVATION OBLIGATION

Company advertising managers and advertising agency account men who provide the service may readily accept that their job is to help marketing achieve its sales objectives. But it is essential to examine this role to see how it can be played. Although it will be covered in detail in a later chapter, it is worth mentioning, too, how important it is in determining how IA&SP must see itself. The role of IA&SP can be compliant and passive or innovative and active.

The employment of promotion in the "marketing mix" across industrial companies varies enormously. The differences are not only between similar companies in the same industry, but across product groups or departments of the same company. The employment of promotion—its quality, quantity, and viability—is profoundly affected by the beliefs, prejudices, habits, traditions, and attitudes of a company's top management, and most particularly by its all-important sales or marketing management. Sales managers' attitudes run the gamut. From the standpoint of the serious and responsible promotion practitioner, these attitudes include the bizarre, the ridiculous, the mystifying, and the frustrating—and are frequently based on specious reasoning or head-in-the-sand obduracy.

To fulfill its role, the IA&SP function must assume the obligation of innovation. If necessary, it must begin with the adjustment of attitudes within the company organization through education and demonstration, the goal being to establish the true perspective for the function in the mind of management. This is perhaps unique to industrial companies. Manufacturers of consumer products rarely either overestimate or underestimate the place of promotion in their marketing programs. In industry, sales managers' attitudes vary tremendously. Their conception goes from the nadir view that "advertising and promotion can't do *anything* to help us sell our products" to the zenith attitude that "advertising" is a magic wand that need only be waved to bring in signed orders. Those who hold the latter view are intensely shocked when the magic wand fails them. Many otherwise astute sales executives who would never order, simply and undifferentiated, $1,000 worth of "lumber," will and do buy $50,000 worth of "advertising."

Management attitude can hobble the effectiveness of industrial promotion to a greater degree than any other single factor. Because it affects every facet of the function, it is more potent than indifferent agency performance, meager in-house capability, or low-ceiling financing. Few practitioners can for long bring initiative and creative thinking to the marketing program when faced with the attitude that the only force that can move the product is the salesman making the calls. Still fewer will prosper if the magic-wand attitude prevails. The proper attitude is the necessary basis for the programs themselves.

The industrial company, by tradition or precedent, may become tied to a particular method of promotion, to advertising in a particular medium, to spending money to keep its name before the public, or to imitating the competition. The management may be so fearful of benefit claims that every specific is milked from its advertising or its printed matter. It may be so conscious of change that copy is confined to generalities while specific sales aids are never produced. The company may be so traditionally oriented to order-filling that any program designed to stimulate different, oblique, or larger scale action is considered too "risky." Influential individuals in the company in functions completely separated from selling and promotion may be so highly regarded that their opinions or their required "okays" impede, deform, or even strangle viable programs.

The professional practitioner knows the truth—that the IA&SP function's capability is real and demonstrable, that it lies midway between the attitude extremes, that it genuinely serves a purpose when it can operate freely in its assigned sphere. A promotion program is a selling tool; it is an effective one when solidly based on a marketing plan that is in turn based on a thorough knowledge of the market. It can be highly potent when assigned its logical share of the selling task. It contributes measurably when it selects the logical communication tools, adapts them to its needs with a high degree of professionalism, and exploits them to the fullest degree in field use.

There is no selling problem in industry where the IA&SP function cannot provide a specific, tangible assist to the sales program.

The innovation obligation thus encompasses: changing internal attitudes in such a way as to assure that the function receives the respect it deserves; freeing the function from confining operational precedent; assuming the initiative to contribute selling tools and soundly conceived, viable programs that demonstrate the function's effectiveness to perform a specific, predetermined task.

MONITORING OBLIGATION

A second obligation of the IA&SP function is to monitor the integrity of the promotion investment. This has many facets. The basic concept, however, is that a promotion program must be solidly based on the market situation, that it must be focused on a specific objective, and that the task assigned or undertaken must be within its proper sphere and its capability. In detailing the innovation obligation, we considered those circumstances where the promotional function is charged with positive action. The monitoring obligation dictates that the function itself under certain circumstances is obligated to reduce or even eliminate the investment of time, effort, and money in promotion programs called for by other functions of the organization, not excluding management.

The monitoring obligation presupposes that the IA&SP practitioner knows from education and experience what an advertising and promotion program can and cannot accomplish. It is assumed that he has adequate knowledge of the seven categories of promotion tools, knows how to create them, knows the purposes to which they are best suited, and knows the strengths and weaknesses of each. It is presumed that he will have sufficient knowledge of the market, the selling problem, and the sales objectives to assess in general the validity of how, where, when, and what kinds of promotion may be effective. Thereafter, his knowledge of his trade and his personal ethics qualify him to maintain the integrity of the company's investment in promotion. He should *repress* promotion when his own expertise tells him this is in the best interests of the company. The circumstances under which an IA&SP

practitioner should feel obligated to revamp, suppress, or refuse to create a promotion program are not as rare as it might first appear.

Management panic and the "urge to act" can be sparked by dozens of causes, including crises in the market, a competitor's move, unforeseen innovation, shifting trends, and government action. Frequently, "promotion" is one of the straws reached for—frantically, compulsively, and, too often, wrongly.

There are three situations where "promotion" is useless as a crutch, where *any* investment in advertising and sales promotion is a waste of money. Even the most massive and creative program will have little perceptible, and certainly no lasting, effect. The circumstances wherein IA&SP is impotent to help sales are in the face of a price disadvantage, in the face of inferior product quality, and in the face of an adverse technological change. It may help save inordinate amounts of effort and expense to look closely at each of these.

PRICE DISADVANTAGE

Pricing, except for undifferentiated commodities, is not an absolute. There are higher- and lower-priced earth-movers, lubricating oils, and factory floorings. Price is set on "value" or on "performance." However, in manufacturing anything—from a wire-drawing machine to a welding torch to a fork lift—operating methods, fixed costs, or labor may establish the cost at a point where the selling price has to be pegged at a higher level than the "value" offered by the competition. Obsolescence of design or function may do the same. In manufacturing a standard chemical, a competitor's new process may produce the same chemical at a higher assay or minus an unwanted impurity. In such instances the price-performance or price-value combination is not as good as what is available elsewhere in the market.

Promotion will not help.

The purchasing agents (and the influential people who enter a transaction) in industry (unlike consumers) do not buy on impulse or emotion. This is one of the facts of life in industrial marketing and promotion. With a large capital purchase or in contracting for a continuous supply of materials, the industrial buyer will be acutely aware of price —and what it buys. If the price-performance offering of the company product is not at least equal to the competition's, no amount of advertising and adroit promotion will disguise the fact. When faced with a promotion task, the practitioner must face the issue of "price for value" as dispassionately and exhaustively as will the buyer before he signs the order. If, on balance, the purchase price is not at least as attractive as the competition's, no investment in promotion should be made. Even the best program will not long hide the facts.

Quality is not entirely related to price. Two heavy-duty transformers do exactly the same work and cost exactly the same. One, however, requires excessive maintenance and after a short time develops higher power losses. Within the world of transformer buyers, this quality deficiency inexorably comes to light. Word of mouth, more swiftly than the unrolling of an advertising campaign, more convincingly than the most effective direct mail, sales literature, or trade exhibit, will put a block in the path of promotion.

"Quality" embraces every facet of the industrial product: its performance, packaging, technical service, warehouse points, storage life, materials, in-plant handling characteristics, installation, efficiency. All of these aspects are weighed in the balance of the purchasing decision. And again, if the offering is not at least as good as the competition's, promotion will not close the gap.

TECHNOLOGICAL CHANGE

In industry there is a constant flux of materials, methods, and systems. It is the result of the unremitting search to lower material costs, to increase productivity, to improve quality, and to save labor. For example, there was the impact of paint sprayers on paintbrushes, then the impact of dip coating on paint sprayers, and now there is the electro-deposition of paint, which will bring about still other changes. For many years the food industry, to take another example, had available only two major food acids, tartaric and citric. In the early 1960s, food-grade fumaric acid came on the scene. For decades rubber-coated fabrics were the only material used in clothing that protected the wearer from water and chemicals. Then a variety of other coatings, including vinyl and urethane, entered the market. Modern tire cord evolved through the intrusions of rayon, nylon, polyester, and steel on cotton. Each of these changes offered its own price-value ratio, its own quality advantages. Each technological change will reach a state of market equilibrium. The trend to such an equilibrium can be *accelerated* by advertising and promotion, but to hold the line against technological change is impossible. To counter a trend, IA&SP is impotent. No amount of promotion will maintain or increase the consumption of paintbrushes, older food acids, rubber coatings, or cotton tire cord in the applications from which changing technology is displacing them. And the astute promotion manager will not attempt to do so.

Price disadvantage, quality, and technological change are conditions of the marketplace and are marketing management problems; they cannot be solved by recourse to promotion. They are outside the province of IA&SP and they constitute insuperable roadblocks to a successful promotion program. If top management or the marketing department expects promotion to save the situation, it is the practitioner's obligation to disabuse them of this idea. By his own awareness, astuteness, and monitoring of the markets, he will maintain the integrity of what the company invests in promotion.

There are many other ways in which promotional expertise should fulfill its monitoring obligation. We shall take up only a few. Most of these stem from the intrusion of unknowledgeable thinking into the area of responsibility that should be reserved to IA&SP expertise. They occur most often in small- to medium-size companies that have previously had little or no industrial promotion guidance from experienced practitioners or that lack an in-house capability.

COMPANY FETISHES

Specialized trade magazines and company mailboxes are full of communications that represent ideas considered important by the sponsoring company but that contribute little or nothing to company sales. The basic criterion for judging all communications must always be: "What does this mean to the buyer?" A producer of factory shelving may be immensely pleased with the efficiency of his metals-inventory handling or the reliability of his order processing. Yet neither of these skills affects the value of what the buyer receives. To use purely internal accomplishments as a promotion base is pointless for advertising or literature. Company brochures that delineate the capability, longevity, and reliability of a supplier have a definite value if the product is complex and costly, and if its performance depends heavily on sophisticated technical know-how. Reputation is essential to the product. However, a "We stand behind the product" brochure or advertising campaign for disposable commodities such as baling wire or crate nails is pointless. In-house methods, skills, and equipment that have no discernible relation to the product value are not impressive to the potential buyer. Company fetishes make sagging promotional platforms. They should be "monitored" out of the promotional communications.

TRADITIONITIS

A sensitive area, but one where monitoring is warranted, is the company's underwriting of advertising for a variety of specious reasons. This "disease" may be chronic. It can show itself in the constant use of a trade association paper with the regular insertion of innocuous advertisements "to support the industry." This practice, however benign, often ignores the fact that the trade association publication is already well filled with solid advertising, is a profitable and effective advertising medium, and no longer has any need for charitable support. Another reason that smacks of the superstitious may be: "to keep our name before the public." Inasmuch as any advertisement that appears in print does indeed keep the company's name before a particular public and costs the same, to make this the prime objective of advertising is akin to buying a fine hand tool to use as a paperweight.

WRONG TOOLS, WRONG DRESS

A company makes a significant product improvement, develops a new product, or produces some highly compelling sales information. Whatever, it calls for a clear, handsome, and well-thought-out sales presentation that may well require something elaborate—perhaps portable audiovisual material for field use. But what may happen is that because the field force traditionally works with a loose-leaf binder of specifications, the new material goes out to the field simply as a new page, conforming to the standard format. Or a company may develop a superbly sophisticated piece of machinery that will be purchased by highly technical engineers. To communicate the achievement, the forward step deserves a special dressing, but gets the wrong kind. The basic sales literature is developed with inappropriate flossy graphics, buries or omits essential information, and may either resemble a circus poster or be as demure as a lingerie promotion from a high-class department store. A company that would not consider employing 80-year-old salesmen or that would not allow its representatives to wear mauve Bermuda shorts may never even consider applying the same discretion to its promotion tools. But the monitoring IA&SP practitioner should. Art for art's sake may be intriguing—but it's not communicative or appropriate.

OVERDIFFUSION

One of the points covered in our later dissection of IA&SP techniques will be fitting the tools and programs to the sales problem. This automatically corrects the error of overdiffusion. Nevertheless, it is also a point of monitoring. Overdiffusion shows itself in two ways: programs that beget an impossible-to-handle response and programs that beget more dross than workable ore.

An advertisement in a publication or a piece of direct mail is expected to *A*ttract, *I*nform, create *D*esire, and spur *A*ction, but with overdiffusion, this old "A.I.D.A." formula tends to be ignored. The action element must be carefully considered. If the action spurred by the advertisement is to the effect of "Send me information on how soybeans can help my business," this is overdiffusion—even if run in a feed magazine or a food processing magazine. This is particularly true, of course, if the seller is offering soya flour as a source of starch for paper coatings or soya oil for making paint.

An offer to supply literature that shows the reader how liquid chlorine can increase his profits will bring in bushels of inquiries. They may include a machine tool designer, a plastics molder, and a corrugated kraft-box fabricator. None will be prospects; none will be pleased or informed. The offer is more than the company can supply.

Overdiffusion works in reverse. "How Mark IV Stampers Increase Efficiency in the Transportation Industry" is a headline that may attract transportation people for whose needs the product is irrelevant. The production chief of a truck assembly plant, the president of a battery manufacturing company, and the designer of hypoid gear axles— all of them connected with transportation—receive a four-color book on a fine automatic tool that makes noncounterfeitable streetcar or subway tokens. The offer is obviously less than has been implied. The more "institutional" the advertisement, the broader the product line, the more encompassing the capability presented—the greater is the danger of overdiffusion.

Thus, in maintaining the integrity of the promotion investment, the IA&SP function's task is twofold. It is charged by ethics and dedication to instigate and create sound promotion to help sell the product. It is obligated by its particular expertise to educate others and establish proper attitudes, to correct inefficient methods, to eliminate wasteful practices.

The foregoing sets the parameters for the visions IA&SP can have of itself. It suggests the scope of responsibility and the orientation in the organization, and specifies the discipline's obligations. Our next concern is to translate the responsibility into methods of practical operation.

2
CREATING THE TOOLS

IA&SP is basically communicating—and as such is both an art and a science. It is a discipline whose role is to create a variety of communication tools that consist of seven types. Each individual one within its genera must be devised to make people think or act in a specific, predetermined way. Persuasive communication is the purpose of all the tools that are the physical output of the IA&SP trade, and most particularly, the combination of tools that make up programs.

The IA&SP discipline encompasses the idea of "audiences," and each of the tools it creates is designed to affect differing quantities of people: two or three of crucial importance, or fifty, or five hundred, or many thousands. It entails the element of psychology, because all the tools that IA&SP creates must be so devised as to make a particular impression on particular types of people and to stimulate a particular desirable reaction. It includes the elements of esthetics and semantics, because what it produces must initially be written and graphically designed to communicate clearly and succinctly and to make the most vivid, lasting, and favorable impression. And most essential, the discipline must be grounded in market knowledge, current sales plans, and a thorough (albeit journalistic) knowledge of the technical products offered.

IA&SP is a technique for communicating ideas to designated people to make them think and act in a specified manner. If you examine it, the discipline closely parallels the art of selling. IA&SP, however, sells not by the actions of a salesman but through one, two, or a combination of the graphic or audiovisual arts. Although it cannot write the order or close a sale, nevertheless it sells through the tools it creates. In some respects, it sells more thoroughly than the salesman.

The communication tools of IA&SP can convey product benefits, service capabilities, and ideas conducive to buying more dramatically, more thoroughly, more succinctly, more convincingly than can a salesman. The tools reduce such ideas to their most "graspable" essence. The tools can reach inaccessible people, instill the buying interest, and presell more purchasing "influentials" at each prospective account than can be simultaneously contacted by a salesman. IA&SP can build a more consistent image of the company or product, one that prevails over the varied personalities of the salesmen. And when good promotion tools are put into the hands of capable field men, when integrated programs are developed in support of personal selling effort, the marketing program reaches its optimum effectiveness.

IA&SP makes its contribution to selling effectiveness through the creation and employment of seven types of tools:

1. Media advertising. Adv
2. Sales literature. Promotion
3. Direct-mail advertising. Prom
4. Physical demonstration items and product exhibits. P~
5. Audiovisuals. P
6. Customer sales presentations. P
7. "Reminder" advertising and goodwill-building items. Adv

Although each of these can be infinitely varied from a creative standpoint, the seven categories make up the boundaries of the IA&SP "art." They are the basic tools the discipline is responsible for and capable of producing. What these turn out to be creatively, how selected combinations of them are developed to make a planned program, and the way they are put to work in the marketing task—this is the key to how well IA&SP assists in the selling job.

Let us briefly look at each of the seven categories. There are benefits and weaknesses with each. They have particular jobs to do. Each is best suited for a specific job, and some are totally unsuited for particular jobs. When the practitioner comes to the all-important task of building a program, these basic strengths and weaknesses are vital in his planning.

MEDIA ADVERTISING

TOOL ONE

In the United States, the industrial marketer has access to more communication channels to particular trades and professions than he would in any other industrial nation. Not only are there publications available that reach specific industries, but there are publications that reach special segments of specific industries. There are specialized and highly technical publications for particular *disciplines,* and their circulation extends horizontally across many industries where that particular discipline is employed. Thus the IA&SP practitioner has available "vertical" publications that penetrate various industries and "horizontal" publications that cover a specific technology or science in all of the industries that employ it. There are publications that reach every level of management and functional interest—from general industrial company and business management to operating plant management, to production management, to maintenance. There are more than 2,000 regular publications and they reach every industry, trade, science, function. Whether the publications are distributed by subscription or by controlled circulation, their publishers provide a wealth of data about them. Reader profiles are provided; readership is documented. So much data is available that it's advisable to consult an experienced agency media specialist in developing a schedule of publications for a specific program. Not only are the best publications to be sought, but the fewest selected for optimum coverage and frequency at minimum cost.

Aside from the task that the "media advertising" tool of an IA&SP program is to accomplish, the following are a few guideposts and rules of thumb in the use of industrial media.

Frequency of appearance is to be preferred over "impact"—unless there are other compelling circumstances, one such being time limit. A one-page advertisement run six times is normally a better investment than a two-page spread run three times.

Appearances in the publication are a better investment than an inordinately high ratio of production costs to media appearance. A four-color advertisement run twice is not as good an investment as a two-color advertisement run six times.

Advertisements in a campaign. The number of advertisements in a media campaign will be determined by the number of product benefits or company facets that must be registered to make the advertised communication complete. If the total communication can be packaged in a single advertisement, a better investment is multiple exposure of this advertisement rather than the frequent creation of a new one. The minimum exposure of a given advertisement should be three or four appearances. There need be no arbitrary maximum, depending on the task of the media campaign.

Point of no return. A reasonable frequency of insertion is essential if the advertisement is to reach all the readers of a given publication. The reasons are obvious: Not all readers read every issue; some every-issue readers may overlook your particular advertisement; some readers may see your advertisement at a critical time when their interest is elsewhere; still others may see the advertisement but take no action until they see it a second or a third time. As a rule of thumb for the economical point of no reduction: in a weekly publication, thirteen appearances a year; in a biweekly, nine; in a monthly, four. Below this, the value of the media investment declines more than the costs saved. In general, it is more advisable to use six appearances a year in two monthlies than three appearances per year in four.

Media advertising is the prime tool for the following tasks.

Company or product image building. Only media advertising can reach an entire audience spectrum at every level of influence simultaneously at such a low per message cost. The "packaging" up of the product message or the company image in an advertisement reduces it to an assimilable, succinct essence. The message reaches the audience in the company of other suppliers who serve the trade. It reaches the audience when individually the readers are in a receptive enough mood to be reading the specialized magazine. Media advertising can give a larger-than-life dimension and build status for a product, service, or company.

To obtain inquiries for sales calls. Media advertising is a low-cost way to make salesmen's calls more productive. Inquiries can be drawn in to distribute sales literature (for preselling) and to request salesmen's calls (for locating interested prospects). Inquiries screened from media advertising presold with literature follow-up can make the salesman's time and travels more productive. The combination of media advertising and literature provides a unique "mechanical" preselling that can enable the salesman to deal directly with individual interests, prices, specific needs, and performance expectations.

To define additional markets. For particular broad-use products, even the best analysis of prospect markets may overlook valuable segments with additional potential. Introductory advertising on short schedules in a variety of media can uncover market segments that are worth additional market study.

To identify and reach buying "influentials." In most industrial sales, a number of "influentials"—that is, people who can affect the outcome of a sale—must be considered. How "weighty" is each? Where does the initial interest in buying start—in the laboratory, on the production floor, in the marketing department, in the front office? "Try and see" schedules in sequentially selected media or "keyed" publications in broad schedules can provide valuable clues as to who are the most potent buying influentials for the product. The advertising reaches "buying influentials" the salesman cannot identify and has never seen. One study reported that only 39 percent of buying influentials are called on by salesmen.

To accelerate a technological trend. If the product to be sold will benefit by the conversion of a whole industry to a new material, new machine, or new process, or by rooting a new method to handle a specific type of operation, media advertising (which will be amply supported by editorial matter) will accelerate a technological change.

Except in very, very special circumstances, media advertising is not a good tool when the prospective buyers number less than 1,000, when the product is an undifferentiated commodity sold through distributors, or when the majority of the potential users are known and accessible, and price is the major selling weapon.

Here is a major guideline in the creation of industrial advertising:

While attention-getting graphics and smart, sophisticated copy are desirable, they are not the imperatives they are in consumer advertising. Neither artwork nor copy style should overpower information.

The readers of industrial publications read for information, not diversion or entertainment. They buy on the basis of facts and logic, not emotion. Industrial advertisements are a major source of information to learn of competent suppliers, discover new materials and unique capabilities, and to keep abreast of technological change. Readers do not have to be "grabbed" by graphics or snared by semantics. They *do* have to be clearly informed and favorably impressed. Bizarre layout, cute illustrations, and catchy copy can often do more harm than good. Industrial decisions to buy, to investigate, or to sample industrial products and services are motivated primarily by need and logic. Conversely, consumer decisions are largely motivated by emotion. This is a fundamental difference between industrial and consumer advertising.

It is a difference that unless understood and observed can mean the difference between an effective media program and a disaster. Smartness for smartness's sake in industrial advertising not only can do the product a disservice, it can make the salesman's job all the harder. An industrial advertisement that offers trade-recognized, realistic benefits in its headline, a demonstration of effectiveness in its illustration, and adequate information in its copy—although it would be judged dull stuff by the consumer-oriented—will do more for the advertiser than the most glittering and sophisticated graphics and copy. If the message is superficial, if the graphics strain for effect, there's a better creative approach, and the practitioner would do well to find it.

SALES LITERATURE

TOOL TWO

It may be quite truthfully said that if one is selling ten-dollar bills for nine dollars, even then it is necessary to have a good, basic piece of sales literature. With industrial products, with the possible exception of the most basic commodities sold on price, effective literature is essential.

There are several basic concepts that apply to industrial sales literature. They relate to use, writing, and graphic production.

Of paramount importance in the creation of this category of sales tool is the need to keep in mind at the outset exactly what the literature is supposed to do, what effect it should have on the reader, and who the reader will be. "Sales literature" covers a wide gamut. It includes the catalog, the product sales book, the brochure, the leaflet, and the technical bulletin.

The preparation of sales literature is greatly simplified if its function is allowed to be the controlling purpose in its preparation. Poor sales literature results when there is more than one purpose or when the purpose is not clearly defined at the start.

It is helpful to separate the function of sales literature into three general purposes: literature designed to sell the reader on buying the product, literature designed to explain thoroughly or educate the buyer on the applications or use of the product, literature necessary for the servicing of the product after it is purchased. The first is intended to create a buying interest in the product or service. It must be assumed that the reader has neither seen the product nor talked to a salesman about it. The second is to deepen initial interest and nurture the buying decision after the reader has shown initial interest—perhaps after he has had contact with a salesman and is already considering buying. The third is to help the buyer make the most satisfactory use of the product or service after he has purchased.

A single piece of literature should rarely attempt to serve all three purposes.

These three basic types should serve as the orientation for the writer and graphic designer who prepare literature for industrial marketing and for the sales executives who request it. The purpose and the audience provide the slant for the writing and the guide for graphics. The foregoing comments constitute a strong recommendation to keep the printed piece "pure" for its designated task. Rarely will a hybrid be thoroughly satisfactory for a bifurcated purpose. And too often, the uninitiated will load printed matter with extraneous information that neutralizes much of its value.

In the field, all three kinds of literature may be used on the same sales call or in answer to the same inquiry. For marketing a given product, only the first type may be necessary, or perhaps the first and third. Each product or service has its own total communication need —for selling and for using fully and properly. This total communication need determines the literature required. A salesman, an engineer, and a technical service man cannot be on hand at all times. Literature is the substitute.

These total communication needs and the controlling purposes must be uppermost in the marketing executive's mind when he addresses himself to sales planning. The same thing applies when the IA&SP practitioner sits down to face a blank sheet of paper.

Since a piece of basic sales literature is required to help sell virtually every product, the following is a simple outline of six "elements" that will help organize the writing task and guide the layout and graphic illustration of sales literature.

Element 1: Cover title (and graphic illustration). This element names the product and communicates immediately its most cogent use benefit(s). It can be thought of as an advertisement lacking only the body copy. Examples:

HODSON SELF-SEAL CRATES
Carry up to a half-ton without fastenings.

LUKENS 2-CYCLE GASOLINE ENGINES
- Fit ½″ to 1″ takeoff shafts!
- Operate on 60 octane gas!
- Deliver 40hp at 750 rpm!

RICHARDSON CONTINUOUS-PROCESS PIPE SEALER
No pressure drop up to 200 psi at 150°C.

LUSTERSHIELD FLEXIBLE TOY VARNISH
- Air-dries in less than 20 minutes!
- Oven-dries at 150°F in 2 minutes!
- Sixteen standard colors!

Element 2: The opening "sell." This element should present clearly, quickly, and convincingly all the use benefits of the product or service. The text should adhere strictly to buyer benefits and not stray to product facts. It should cover every possible use benefit that can influence a decision to buy. This selling element should use terminology familiar to the trade and draw its value judgments from sources well grounded in the practical technology of the market.

Element 3: The "explanation" of product or service. This section should describe the product in every detail that is of interest to the buyer. Here is the place to give all the product facts. It serves as the backup to the use benefits. It tells the reader exactly what he is buying. Basically, this is the "what it is" and "why it is good" element. Here appears the complete explanation of the product (or service) and pertinent data on construction, constitution, operation, performance.

Element 4: The "how to use" or "how it works." This section describes the way to use, data on installation, methods of application, directions for servicing—all the *general* information that the buyer will need to know that will affect his buying decision. It can cover space needs, dispensing devices, floor support, building modification, utility services, operations, processes, and fittings. This element should convey all that's involved in what the product will do.

Element 5: The "precautions." This section covers any warnings of misuse, installation hazards, incompatibility notice, handling or operating hazards, storage considerations, maintenance needs, or safety precautions. It should provide information that guides the user in the safe handling, storage, operation, and use of the product. It should not be alarming, but it should be realistic and forthright. And eagerness to avoid liability should not spread the information to other elements or salt the sell with precautions.

Element 6: The "assurance" element. This can cover technical service, kinds of users, recommendations for applications, operations, companies or industries using, warranty, standard-of-performance ratings. Here is given all the information that assures the reader that what has been described has ample backup and that performance will be as presented.

The values of adhering to this simple outline are many. Few other skeleton outlines that can be set up will prove as serviceable. The major benefits are: The development of the communication maintains continuity; the most important impressions come first and the others in logical order; the major facets of complete communication are all accounted for; and each element of the literature remains "pure"—un-muddied with matter irrelevant to the particular purpose of each section. The outline will serve as the skeleton for a single-fold leaflet and for a 48-page book. Most pertinent, an artist will find the copy organized and easy to lay out; the reader will get a complete concept of what is offered for sale. Although each section may have subheads, the six-element division virtually demands six section headlines, as:

1. *Title Element*

JOHNSON SELF-LOCK SCREWS
HOLD SHEET-METAL CONSTRUCTION
TIGHTER THAN RIVETS

2. *Sell Element (Headline)*

40% FEWER FASTENERS NEEDED
WHEN YOU USE JOHNSON SELF-LOCK!

3. *Explanation Element (Headline)*

JOHNSON SELF-LOCKS ARE ZIRCON ALLOY
WITH PATENTED "GRAB" DESIGN

4. *How-to Element (Headline)*

PRESS IN—TWIST TWICE

5. *Precaution Element (Headline)*

USE JOHNSON SELF-LOCKS FOR EVERY JOB
NOT REQUIRING IMMERSION IN SEA WATER

6. *Assurance Element (Headline)*

CHECK THIS LIST OF APPLICATIONS WHERE
JOHNSON SELF-LOCKS ARE CUTTING COSTS

The amount of body copy in each element is dictated by the communication task. In industrial literature, layout must accommodate copy, so the quantity of text in each "element" is not material. It can be short and succinct or it can be as long as necessary. The most important factor in preparing basic sales literature is to keep each element pure.

A helpful device for the writer (and layout artist) is the "breakout" of either highly important or purely ancillary material from the running narration of the body copy. If a series of figures, a list of facts, or a data comparison series is needed, it can be broken out as a separate copy box, made into a graph, or presented as a table. These breakouts can then be used in the layout as graphic illustrations in the same manner as other picture elements.

The breakout of material, however, is the *writer's* responsibility. The layout artist should not be expected to understand the material so well that he can "edit" the writer's manuscript. On the other hand, the writer will help the artist immeasurably if he prepares a "rough" from his manuscript. This is a very crude layout that merely indicates the importance of various copy elements and illustrations for their sizing, their logical positioning with respect to the body copy of the text, and the relative weights of headlines and subheads.

EDUCATION OR EXPLANATION LITERATURE

For literature whose task is to fulfull the second purpose—that is, printed pieces designed to explain thoroughly or to instruct the buyer on the applications or use of the product—a practical guide outline is simple.

1. Title—which explains this exact purpose. Examples:

    THE 40 MAJOR USES OF
    HODSON SELF-SEAL CRATES

    POWER ALL THESE MACHINES
    WITH A LUKENS ENGINE

    HERE'S WHERE RICHARDSON PIPE SEALERS CAN
    GUARD YOUR PROCESS

2. A *short* recap "sell" element.
3. A clear, topical sequence of the complete "where or how to use" information.

Literature whose task is to fulfill the third purpose—that is, information for handling or servicing of the product after it is purchased—should eliminate any "selling" element. It should be lucid and to the point—and the graphics should be kept as simple and uncluttered as possible. It should cover every aspect of the subject, under distinct topical headings. If the second product example given above were to be used, the service literature for the Lukens engine might have this outline:

LUKENS 2-CYCLE GASOLINE ENGINE INSTALLATION AND MAINTENANCE

Topic 1: Positioning in the Equipment

Topic 2: Mounting and Vibration Damping

Topic 3: Ventilation and Access Points

Topic 4: Engine Controls

Topic 5: Fuel and Lubrication Requirements

Topic 6: Break-in and Maintenance

Topic 7: Parts List

In producing service literature, the practitioner should always be alert to the direct customers' *entire* requirements for information. With many industrial products or materials that are components of a finished product, the initial buyer needs information that he, in turn, can pass on to his customer. In our example, a power-mower manufacturer buying the Lukens engine must instruct his distributors and the ultimate homeowner buyer on the engine's operating characteristics. Consequently, the producer of service literature should be alert to the pass-on needs of the direct customer. Whenever possible, the service literature should be prepared so that the direct customer's own service or selling task requires only minimum effort on his part.

Obviously, if all three kinds of literature are necessary for a given product, in appearance they should have a "family" resemblance. When laid side by side they should look as if they belonged together. A competent artist, so instructed, can achieve this resemblance by—among other techniques—using the same type styles and matched colors, handling the product name and the company trademark in exactly the same way wherever they appear, and using graphics that relate.

Small and medium-size industrial companies with no professional agency and in-house IA&SP capability frequently hand out manuscripts for literature directly to a printer. The results are rarely satisfactory. Expertise is essential in every step of literature production: writing, graphic design and layout, and final print production. While large and even small printers will "arrange type and pictures," the final printed piece will invariably be substandard in appearance. A printer's job is printing, not design and layout. If there is no one in-house with the expertise to supervise or no advertising agency available for graphic design, all written material that is to be printed should first be designed and laid out for reproduction by a competent commercial artist experienced in designing *industrial* literature. It costs the same to set badly chosen type styles in bad layout and to run the printing press with poor page design as it does for an expertly designed brochure. The artist's fee is well worth it cost.

In writing technical product literature, do not underestimate the reader's intelligence or overestimate his knowledge—but avoid telling him $2 \times 2 = 4$.

DIRECT MAIL

TOOL THREE

Direct mail is the tool most suitable for reaching a relatively limited number of buying influences whose personal identities and locations are known. It is also valuable as an auxiliary to media advertising to bring intense promotional pressure on a selected number of highly potent prospects in an audience spectrum where relatively few account for the largest consumption of the product. Its strengths lie in the quantity of information it can deliver, the dramatic fashion in which it can do so, and the fact of its being delivered to a concentrated audience. Direct mail has a high assurance of message registration. Its weaknesses will almost always be in either the customer list or misguided creativity.

Volumes are available on the techniques of using direct mail. For our purposes in strictly industrial promotion, much of the basic general consumer know-how is applicable. But, as with media advertising, there are major differences. It is impossible to lay down comprehensive guidelines for industrial direct mail since these vary depending on the kind of product, its position in its marketing evolution, and the task to be achieved. Yet a few guidelines are generally applicable.

To begin with, a simple, well-written, personally addressed sales letter, mailed first class and attached to or offering the basic sales literature, is one of the most effective kinds of industrial direct mail. Its strength depends on the completeness and accuracy of the list. Although men in industry receive many mailings, "letters" are read and acknowledged. Because it is accepted practice for companies to exchange information by letter, personal letters, sent first class, will attract far more interest and get far more attention than even the most highly imaginative direct mail pieces—all other factors being equal. A good letter written specifically to you, personally and correctly addressed, can be most compelling. One that betrays itself as a device obviously loses its effect.

Weakness in the quality of the list can partly be compensated for by (1) wider diffusion of a mailing over a broader spectrum of names, and (2) by the impact value of the mailing piece.

For industrial use, the term "impact value" requires elaboration. Flossiness, shimmering poster type, fluorescent inks, clever copy, gimmick folds, string pulls, or other graphic drama in the "art for art's sake" tradition are a waste. The same taste, the same appeal to logic, the same succinctness, and the same provision of to-the-point information that impart strength to industrial media advertising apply to direct mail. The test: Is the graphic device functional? A mailing piece bedecked with ribbons and bows, songbirds and pop-outs, added purely for the sake of the unusual, will not justify its cost. If the cleverness amplifies the information, gets across the message more quickly, drives home the point with greater emphasis—then graphic drama can justify its cost. However, the production cost of the mail-out piece in most instances far exceeds its diffusion, and any "testing" can only come after the fact. In the writing and designing of direct mail, the purpose of the promotion, the quality of the list, the product information value, the type of communication to be made, and the expected action all govern its creation. In the face of large audiences and weak lists, its value in relation to media advertising must be carefully evaluated.

PHYSICAL DEMONSTRATION ITEMS AND PRODUCT EXHIBITS

TOOL FOUR

Physical sales tools can be one of the most potent factors in making the field salesman effective. Nothing is more communicative than demonstration; nothing is more convincing than seeing, feeling, handling, trying. The IA&SP practitioner can find no more rewarding way to invest his creativity than by providing the sales force with the "devices of conviction." These range from easy-to-use "sample kits" to "before" and "after" samples; from physical examples of test results to significant "parts" of the product being sold. Obviously, the demonstration aids provided will vary enormously across the span of industrial products. However, these principles apply:

1. Supply the field force with *something* physical.
2. Provide it in a form easy to carry and use.
3. Make certain it demonstrates something significant—either in the product or what the product does.
4. Design the demonstration piece so that what it has to say is immediately and dramatically apparent.

The value of something to handle, feel, and examine as a conversation piece can hardly be overstressed. Aside from samples of the product itself, the following series of types of "physicals" can serve as a creative checklist for the kinds of items that can give the field salesmen talking points.

Examples of Work the Product Does (Performance Tests)

For glues	A multiple-deck sandwich of dissimilar materials bonded together
For fasteners	See how easy to tighten
For lubricants	Examine this surface after 10,000 hours' rubbing
For dispensers	The ten equal volume of dispensed portions
For detergents	Comparison wash test
For metal fencing	Weather-exposure samples
For coatings	Comparisons with other plated, painted, cured-finish samples "before" and "after" exposures

Significant Construction Examples

• Welding, riveting, resin-bonded material samples.
• Samples of actual material used in critical parts.
• A jigsaw-puzzle type of assembly.
• A sequenced overlay artwork diagram buildup.
• Samples of actual components—from handles to springs to meters.

Models and Critical Parts

- Scale miniatures of large capital equipment.
- Models of selected working parts.
- Layout diagrams with cut-out scale modules of product.
- Actual significant parts—from bearings to portions of control panels, sample wiring, a power switch, a container's lock or closure.

The possibilities are virtually endless. The generalizations only serve to emphasize the point that invariably there is some way that creative thinking, when applied hard enough and in collaboration with a qualified technologist and field salesman, can devise something physical that will give the field salesman a specific talking point. Providing such talking points will make a significant contribution to the sales program.

Trade exhibits are salesmen's demonstrations on the grand scale. In the creation of exhibits, there are two goals: to attract heavy attendance and to communicate and register the product benefits after attendance is secured.

Exhibits, like salesmen's demonstration kits, like every tool IA&SP creates, start out with a blank sheet of paper. Each must be *written,* no matter how rough the draft. Most particularly, in creating either a salesman's demonstration kit or a trade exhibit, the legends, tags, signs, banners, and headlines must be written out *first.* This is the starting point. They may be changed, revised, added to, deleted, reworded—but the practitioner should have words on paper. And most particularly so for a trade exhibit.

The sales and technical "communication" of the exhibit will of course depend on the product. However, the same principles that apply to a media advertisement and a salesman's kit apply to the exhibit. As much demonstration as possible should be provided—of the product itself or the work it does. If long-life valves are the product, exhibiting a new valve side by side with one that has been 1,000 hours in strong sulfuric acid is more impressive than the beautiful new valve bathed in changing-hued colored lights. If the product is a super strong link-chain for conveyor systems, a yard of quarter-inch chain supporting a pendulum-swinging ton weight is a more valuable exhibit than the polished chain under jeweler's glass on blue velvet. Legends and texts should be short and succinct. The greater the degree of visitor participation that can be built into the exhibit, the more deeply the communication registers.

Attracting attendance is largely the province of exhibit-building specialists. Like agency art directors, they have a repertoire of creative ideas that they will furnish their clients. Clients, however, should feed in ideas, because many of the best ideas have come from client companies. However, defining the technical communication sought and the impression to be registered is the sole obligation of the company and the IA&SP practitioner. These basic elements should be written down at the outset when creating a trade exhibit or creating a field salesman's sample or demonstration kit.

AUDIOVISUALS

Tool Five

The audiovisual sales aid as one of the seven generic tools of selling is a distinct creation in itself; in its *use* it can enter the categories of the salesman's demonstration kit and the sales presentation. Actually it is a particular graphic mode applicable to the work performed by tool categories 4 and 6. It can also function as media advertising. However, from a creative and application standpoint, it is well to consider it by itself.

Audiovisuals range from the simple slide presentation amplifying a live speaker's commentary up through every technical gradation, starting with an added taped or recorded commentary, to the types of production that use combinations of slides, movies, multiple screens, and stereophonic sound. For our purposes—categorizing the tools, examining their fitness for specific tasks, and setting down some basic guidelines for their creation—we can treat the subject of audiovisuals quite briefly.

Their "impression" potential is tremendous; their communication capability limitless. The only question is how "capturable" is the audience. A highly effective color and syncsound motion picture that magnificently demonstrates the use benefits of high-pressure plastic pipe versus cast steel cannot work its magic unless it can be adequately shown. If technical meetings can be arranged, if as many as a half-dozen or ten influentials at key prospective accounts can be convened, a movie of this nature can be justified. It will thus be used as a selling tool, a more potent (though more restricted) instrument than the sales brochure. A moving picture as a training aid to tell how to use the product after it has been purchased can be invaluable. The criteria for creation and investment again boil down to the questions "What is it supposed to do?" and "To whom is it addressed?" and "Can the influentials be collected for the showing?" A sound-slide series or a movie that can be used either across a desk or in a room accommodating a larger audience will obviously have greater probability for exposure because of its dual utility. The use of the tool must be judged on the basis of the job it must do, the potential for exposure, and the cost of the tool in relation to other modes of communication. For selling $5-million airplanes that require acceptance by perhaps a hundred influentials who will be eager to investigate every detail of construction and performance, the most elaborate audiovisual can be justified. For selling diesel engine gaskets that are bought on price by single purchasing agents at 300 locations, a film might well be promotional overloading.

For audiovisuals, as for trade exhibits, specialists are required for final production. However, for the most efficient development of story line and a minimum of false starts, it is the job of the IA&SP practitioner *to write out* a basic and complete briefing of what the audiovisual is to communicate, the material it is to cover, and the *impression* it is to make on the audience. This briefing and one story conference will save a spate of story conferences and perhaps several drafts by the specialist writer-producer.

SALES PRESENTATIONS

TOOL SIX

Sales presentations fall into two classes: (a) a communication tool that the salesman carries to many accounts, and (b) highly individualized communications prepared for a selected few target accounts or for use on a critical call on a single account.

The value of the multiple-use, across-the-board presentation is that it tends both to lift and level out the performance of salesmen. The presentation can be in the form of an audiovisual for desk-showing equipment. More frequently it is most useful as a lettered, illustrated "flip-over." It can be any size convenient for handling.

In the preparation of sales presentations, the technique is to introduce a single idea per page, with minimum copy, in logical and persuasive sequence. The title page should consist of the specific idea that the whole of the presentation is to implant. Examples:

HOW HODSON SELF-SEAL CRATES CAN
SAVE YOU 40% IN SHIPPING COSTS

WHY A LUKENS 2-CYCLE MOTOR PERMITS
YOU TO EXTEND YOUR WARRANTY PERIOD

WHERE RICHARDSON PIPE SEALER CUTS
INSPECTION MAINTENANCE COSTS

The next element after the title should be a succinct recap of the product (or proposition) benefits in not more than 25 to 30 words. Then in succession, *one idea per page,* the presentation can present the evidence, the supporting data, the logical unveiling of all factors that support the keynote idea. Copy should be limited, and graphs, tabular material, diagrams, and illustration should be clear and visually communicative. Each page should be readable in a few seconds. The idea communicated by each page should be complete. Although the salesman using the presentation will amplify the ideas that unfold one by one, in no instance should the visual be written simply as a memory aid for points of the salesman's speech. What the viewer *sees* will register more strongly than what he hears, so the flip-over must communicate a complete idea per page, or per element.

In a flip-over—for general use or a special restricted use—the graphics as well as the copy should aim for rapid registration. The voice and mood of the verb should be consistent throughout—unless deliberately changed on certain pages of the presentation for emphasis or special effect.

The following is a general guide to applying these principles.

(Cover)

RICHARDSON PIPE SEALER REDUCES YOUR COSTS FOUR WAYS

(Page 1)

1. SIMPLIFIED SUPPLY INVENTORY

A single sealer serves the *whole plant.* You can use Richardson on piping for water, steam, aromatic solvents, hydrocarbons, acids, and alkalies.

(Page 2)

2. LESS MAINTENANCE

Monthly inspections can be *dropped.* Richardson sealer stays pliable, resists heat embrittlement, solvation, and creep. Six- or ten-month inspections are standard practice.

(Page 3)

3. FASTER JOINTING

Piping assembly time *drastically cut.* Richardson sealer is soft, pliable, tacky. One swipe in each direction with a 4″ putty knife coats a 10″ pipe.

(Page 4)

4. EASY SECTION REPLACEMENT

Old piping flanges separate *clean*. Richardson sealer resists caking for 3 years at 250°F. No grinding, scraping, buffing when new sections are laid in your system.

Here is why. . . .

(Page 5)

RICHARDSON PIPE SEALER IS THE *ONLY* SEALER THAT:

- Takes 250 psi at 375°F.
- Resists embrittlement for up to 3 years.
- Spreads at room temperature on any metal.
- Requires no scraping for renewal.

(Page 6)

RICHARDSON SEALER SAVES CONSTRUCTION, INSPECTION, REPAIR TIME IN THESE TYPES OF INSTALLATION:

- Continuous process chemical plants.
- Soap and detergent manufacturing.
- Food processing.
- Resin, paint, adhesive cooking.
- Pharmaceutical formulation.
- Steam power plants.
- Petroleum cracking.

The flip-over should continue in this way for each concept necessary for the total communication.

A sales presentation should package the sales "punch" so that it is communicated in its entirety, delivered in logical sequence, couched in the most persuasive and convincing language, and presented simply. It is the sales proposition reduced to its essence. It is for this reason that critical calls on single accounts can be made more effective with the aid of a flip-over or slide presentation. Size and format will depend on the size of the audience. Presentations for 6 to 12 people can be typed and giant photostats made or lettered in speedball. Particular sheets in the sequence can carry mounted pockets for holding literature or technical data that warrants later reference and distribution at a particular point in the sequence of presentation. And, for lasting registration, 8½" x 11" versions of the presentations can be prepared and left behind with the participants at the conclusion of the meeting.

A key checkpoint in the writing of a sales presentation for general use or for a pivotal call is the tone. The safest can be described as logical, factual, and sincere—even though it's emphatic. The emotional response stimulated by an ill-considered tone can be disastrous. Although the experienced practitioner will not require a warning on this score, the following intentionally bizzare examples in the form of sales presentation titles should illustrate what to avoid:

RICHARDSON SEALER SAVES MONEY FOR THE SMARTEST PROCESS PLANT BUYERS—HOW ABOUT YOU?

GET ON RICHARDSON SEALER'S MONEY-SAVING BANDWAGON NOW!

THE LONGER YOU OPERATE WITHOUT RICHARDSON SEALER, THE MORE MONEY YOU THROW AWAY.

IF YOU LIKE TO SEE PIPEFITTERS SCRAPING FLANGES— DON'T SPECIFY RICHARDSON SEALER.

Oddly enough, a tone that might be permissible in an advertisement can backfire in a face-to-face presentation. It is possible that a flamboyant company with communications directed broadside through media advertising at a widespread audience can do things there it can't do where personal sensitivities are involved. In presentations it is safest to talk clearly but quietly.

REMINDER ADVERTISING AND GOODWILL BUILDERS

TOOL SEVEN

This category includes the familiar "giveaways" that can range from the ordinary book matches that carry the company name to effective (and costly) devices.

In industry, small giveaways and reminder-advertising items are widely used. Their value is dependent on the imagination and creativity involved. While suppliers of reminder-advertising items offer a full range, some of the most effective can be created by the IA&SP practitioner, and especially so when they relate to a planned program.

As a general basis for employing this category of tool, we can say that effectiveness is in direct relation to these attributes: (1) novelty,

(2) usefulness, and (3) close relation to product, sales benefit, or impression to be registered.

A familiar type of reminder-advertising item that fulfills these three conditions would be the pocket calculators or information-retrieval devices in the form of slide rules or discs of the type created by Graphic Calculator Company, Perrygraf, and other producers. A device that provides information or saves time on any aspect of the use, installation, maintenance, analysis, testing, or cost estimation involving your product or service is an excellent reminder-advertising item. And any tool, instrument, machine gauge, quick test, nomograph, or reference table that can be provided to effectively serve these purposes will be well received. Examples:

• A major manufacturer of acetyl salicylic acid for the manufacture of aspirin tablets designs and produces for the proprietary drug industry a spring-activated, tablet-hardness tester and a vernier-calibrated, tablet-thickness gauge.

• A producer of boiler-water conditioning chemicals devises a special test kit that provides simple, rapid tests for critical factors in boiler water.

• A producer of corrugated board provides a slide graph that calculates the board stock needed for given quantities of packing cases of various dimensions, indicating waste and directions for die-cuts and scoring.

Also effective purely as goodwill builders are items made from the product being sold that demonstrate one of its benefits—albeit entirely out of context. Examples might be: a manufacturer of conveyor belting making up strips of the material as a car-tow strap; a producer of castings making up a miniature anvil for a home-workshop tool bench; a manufacturer of asbestos-pipe-covering making up "mitts" for handling hot objects.

The criterion for creating reminder-advertising items is how useful the item can be to the recipient in relation to the industrial product for sale. From this standpoint, such items as ballpoint pens, calendars, book matches, and letter openers rank low on the totem pole of effectiveness.

These, then, are the seven kinds of tools that the IA&SP practitioner can create. What tools are created, how they relate, and how they are put to use—to decide such questions is the task of promotion planning and program building. A hammer is a tool; but there are claw hammers, tack hammers, ball hammers, sledge hammers, and pile drivers. A sales task may require one specialized tool or it may require three or four, each designed for one part of the job. No tool is of any absolute value; its *raison d'être* is simply the job or part of the job it is expected to do. And no single tool will take the place of all the others that are needed. Each is to be judged on the basis of what it contributes to the program as a whole. What the total program is to be and what tools it requires are considerations that depend entirely on the promotion task, the job that IA&SP is assigned to do in the marketing program.

3

THE TASKS IA & SP CAN HANDLE

We can say categorically that the IA&SP function can help solve any industrial product-selling problem. The discipline can contribute its particular expertise to fit the promotion assist into the marketing plan, can provide logical tools to optimize the effectiveness of general field selling, and can furnish powerful ammunition to increase the impact of critical calls on highly important "target" accounts. The value obtained from the discipline is limited only by the capability of its practitioners (as with any specialist calling) and by the marketing methodology. This sweeping statement is based on the definition that IA&SP is a technique for making people think and act in a predetermined way. The "people" are the many or few influentials in a given industrial audience. The predetermined way they are to think and act is based on analysis of the sales problem. The means by which the thought and action are to be stimulated are programs fitted out with various combinations of the seven selling tools.

Before making a rough demarcation of the types of tasks IA&SP can undertake, we can detail a number of peripheral jobs that can benefit by the practitioner's professional touch. Often, these are handled without a thought as to whether they could benefit by the professionalism available from the promotion department or the advertising agency. Some of these tasks are described in the following paragraphs.

PLANT SIGNS, ROLLING STOCK INSIGNIA, STATIONERY, LABELS

Two criteria apply to these different vehicles of communications: consistency and good design. Take a fictional company name: Standard Drill & Tool Company. Typography can make this industrial manufacturer's name suggest an elite boutique, an Indian reservation, or a solid industrial company offering steel products. The "image" of the company is displayed to the industrial business community it serves and to the general public by the plant and office signs, by the labels on the packed-out products, by the vehicles that transport them, and by the correspondence that deals with the business of selling and servicing them. It is at once apparent that the styling of the company name should be consistent with the type of business; that once set it should be sacrosanct and the same everywhere. While a letterhead styling is rarely changed and product labels once prepared are simply reprinted as needed, the lack of consistency between what appears on labels, stationery, plant signs, rolling stock, and in advertisements and literature can often be shocking when samples of the various items are examined side by side. This area is peripheral to applying IA&SP to the selling problem—but it is an area of communication. The professional practitioner can establish styling to bring about consistency, and thereafter can maintain the consistency by adhering to the styling in the communication tools produced.

CREATION OF TRADEMARKS

Trademarks can be a most valuable asset to a company; they can also be pointless obfuscations. The value of a trademark is not the name itself, but the value built into the name by advertising, by broad and continued use, and by general recognition and association. To take extreme hypothetical examples:

The Hammond Company is a maker of special food-wrapping machines. It develops a patent-protected machine for wrapping caramels, and quickly sells six machines to two of the candy industry's ten caramel producers. It then wants to "sell the whole field." It searches frantically for a "trademark."

There is no necessity for or value in a trademark for the machine! To designate it as a "Twis-Fla" (registered trademark, Hammond Co.) machine is a waste of time, effort, and money. Rather than rechristen the machine, it is far better to peg the proprietary registration and recognition value to the *company* name with a fully descriptive phrase, such as: "The Hammond Flat-Twist Caramel Wrapper."

The engineers who developed the machine might feel highly indignant and bring forth the specious reasoning that it is a patented wrapping device and should be "protected" with a trademark. What is forgotten is that patents already protect the machine. Excellence lies in what the machine does, and the proprietorship of this is the Hammond Company's own design. If another machine maker produces a flat twist caramel wrapper, it cannot be a "Hammond" machine. Hence, the recognition of excellence is recognition of the *Hammond* machine—and there is no need to bother with building it around something like "Twis-Fla."

A second area where a trademark is superfluous is with commodities that are not a bit different from other suppliers' materials. Typical examples might be a specific melting-point paraffin, a specific boiling-point toluene, a standard-strength sulphuric acid. Buyers of such commodities are accustomed to buying paraffin, toluene, and sulphuric. To call these "Melwa," "Solvut," and "Acidex" is simply to obscure their identities. If there is a special purity, high assay, or use benefit in which advertising money will be invested in order to proclaim that the particular product is *not* like the standard commodity, a trademark may be justified. But not unless the difference is real, recognizable, and valued by the astute industrial buyer. Simply tagging an undifferentiated product with a trademark will not gain greater acceptance. Indeed, if an industrial company enjoys an outstanding reputation, it is often more valuable to use the company name than a trademark. "Du Pont Shellac" or "Sherwin-Williams Shellac" would have a greater likelihood of acceptance than a Jones Paint Co. shellac, even though it bore some imaginative trademark, such as "Fyrelyte."

Where a trademark is justified and where value will be built into it with advertising investment, three attributes should be sought in creating the name—aside from its legal availability. The name should be easy to remember, easy to pronounce (and hard to mispronounce), and it should connote the application or a "use benefit" of the product.

Since descriptive terms, such as "No Flame," "Surface Seal," and "Grasp," are rarely, if ever, registerable, the creator of trademarks is forced to coin words. And from this necessity can come a Pandora's box of troubles. At least a few of them can be scotched by observing the following guidelines.

A newly coined word will appear strange and alien to almost everyone who sees it for the first time—with the exception of the one who has racked his brains to coin it. Thus to try to arrive at a final decision on a single proposed trademark (prior to legal search) by committee is an invitation to dissension. A more practical way is to gather as many suggestions as possible from whatever sources are available—but with at least one creative writer acting as collector, author, and editor. Ideally, he should be an IA&SP practitioner. He should screen out all names that do not possess all three of the previously mentioned attributes, a screening that should result in various names of fair to excellent quality. From this, the marketing executive and the promotion practitioner should settle on a list of not less than six. Any one of this list must be acceptable. The one that is found to be legally available will be used. The list is then submitted for the normal search and registration-application procedure. If the "acceptable" list should include as many as eight or ten names, the chances of availability are that much greater.

The principle of limiting the final choice to one marketing executive and one creative promotion man is essential for both efficiency and trademark quality. Too often, poor trademarks are adopted simply because they are available, or because they are the ones that squeeze through too wide an opinion screening, or because a creative writer (whose professional business is words) never gets involved. Personal reactions to coined words will reflect personal associations with the syllables used. Some coined words can contain syllables that are uniformly distasteful, such as "Cancerette," "Bastorex," "Retchol," and so forth. However, practically any coined word will encounter many rejections that are personal and nothing more. The more "approvals" or "rejections" sought, the more individual rejections for wholly personal reasons. Thus trademarks decided on by committee, or composed by lawyers or engineers without screening, or chosen because of availability only, are all practices it is wise to avoid. Stick to: (a) collection, (b) creation and editing out a long list meeting the three requirements, (c) screening by the one marketing executive responsible for selling, and (d) final legal screening of the "any of these will serve" list. This will not only prove the most efficient method for arriving at trademarks of good quality, it will also insure the aptness of the names. "Chiffonette," for example, is more likely to be attached to a fine filter cloth than to roller bearings, and "Lustrolac" to a dipcoat finish than to a tool grinder. Names like "Poono," "By-Liq," or "Quem," with the sole virtue of availability, will not ever be dignified by an appearance in type.

GENERIC TASKS OF THE TRADE

A definitive itemizing of the ways IA&SP can help sell products is a virtual impossibility, for the number of variables across complex industries is far too great. Among others, these variables include type of product, type of market, capital purchase, continuous supply, position in the market, position in the technology, company stature in a trade, company posture in a specific market, marketing objectives, and type of sales organization. Just how IA&SP is applied for maximum effectiveness will depend entirely on the problem that emerges from an analysis of the company's marketing position. However, we can outline a general catalog of typical tasks that IA&SP can perform. They are the generic tasks of the trade.

A product in its marketing progression can be thought of as going through three phases.

Phase 1. This is the period when the product is new to the trade or when it has been "re-newed" with a significant improvement. The major task of marketing here is to communicate the existence of the product and its most sales-compelling use benefits to all buying influentials in a particular market. The Phase 1 problem is essentially to "let 'em know you've got the product and why it's good." The action sought is to establish awareness, to locate company prospects and individuals within the companies who should be interested, and to stimulate prospects' sampling, trying, evaluating, or requesting more information.

A given product, such as a special chemical oxidation-inhibitor for bar soap, may have only one market: soap manufacturers. Inasmuch as there are not more than 50 soap manufacturers in the industry, the Phase 1 period for this single market would be relatively short. Conversely, there might be a product such as a time-labor-material–cost tabulator for building-contractor foremen, whose market might number in the hundreds of thousands. The Phase 1 period for such a product might last for many years, indeed might never go into Phase 2 in its marketing life. A third product might be an industrial wire binder. This type of product might have a market among printing firms supplying string tags, a second among wire companies supplying connecting leads, and a third among producers of artificial flowers. The wire binder will pass through the Phase 1 period in each market.

With a product in the Phase 1 period, IA&SP programs can play a key role in making the product and its use benefits known, getting interested prospects to identify themselves, optimizing the sales calls that follow up the leads, and defining other markets or market segments for the product.

Phase 2. After a product has been in the trade for a given time and established its value and market, a competitive product enters the picture. It may be virtually identical. In Phase 2, then, the major problem of marketing is to secure the share of business necessary to defeat the competition. There are literally dozens of ingenious ways IA&SP can help in the problem of doing so—in the absence of price cutting. If the product is one that is regularly supplied—such as a raw material—the practitioner can create a special service attendant on the product, develop programs designed to reinforce repeat buying, create promotions designed to favorably influence buying personalities, and mount intense-pressure programs at key accounts. If the product is a single, spot-capital purchase, the practitioner can build an aura around the company as back-up to the product, emphasize a particular facet of the product that exceeds the value of the competitor's, build up the value of the back-up technical service, create an image of greater dependability and wider acceptance, or reassure the buyer by citing preference over a longer period by more users. Similar programs and special sales tools can be developed to promote second and third purchases of capital items.

Phase 3. Assuming that the first two phases of the marketing evolution are successful, that all prospective buyers in a given market know of the product's existence and its merits, and that a predominant market share has been wrested from the competition, the marketing evolution moves into Phase 3. This is the point at which the only way to increase sales is to expand one or more of the end markets into which the product goes. Thus the marketing problem is to expand the sales of or multiply the markets for the product's primary direct customers.

A typical instance might involve a product such as sheet aluminum that is being sold to a variety of regional container makers who produce and sell aluminum cans for motor oil, beer, and salted nuts. The primary aluminum-sheet marketer can enlist IA&SP programs in the task of getting more oil companies, more brands of beer, and more packagers of salted nuts to convert to aluminum containers, or, if the customer himself is energetically doing this, the primary producer can aim his expansion promotion at such products as antifreeze, soft drinks, and paint. In Phase 3, the task is to help your customers or customers' industry find more business for existing lines and/or an entirely new spectrum of potential outlets.

> *One of the major factors in employing IA&SP effectively is to know what "phase" of marketing the product is in and to design the promotion program accordingly.*

Proceeding without regard for the marketing phase can lead to sad misdirection of promotion effort. It is most frequently found in connection with a new technological trend. Take the following fictional but typical example:

A translucent plastic film is developed that is more economical, safer, and lower in cost than glass panes for covering commercial green houses. Within a short time, two producers enter the market. Both launch media advertising campaigns to the greenhouse-operating market, but with advertisements designed to "beat the competition." Each trumpets the superiority of his particular film. However, the conversion from glass has barely started! Instead of a Phase 2 approach, a Phase 1 approach by both producers is far more warranted. There is much more volume in building the market than in fighting for a bigger competitive share.

In citing some of the kinds of tasks IA&SP can do, any general listing suffers from the inevitable weakness of generalization. Without reference to a specific sales problem, a bare description of capabilities becomes a catalog without illustrations, sizes, dimensions, or prices. Tasks that IA&SP can do become real, their value becomes self-evident, and the tools required become logical only when the function is considered in relation to a marketing problem and a specific sales objective. Nevertheless, for the guidance of marketing planners and IA&SP practitioners, even a bare listing can have value. In effect, a listing establishes the wide parameters within which the IA&SP discipline can operate. It can make sales and marketing executives fully aware of what the profession can contribute to their marketing program. The listing can shake the negative conviction that persists in some industrial companies that "advertising can't help us sell our product." While it may be true that purely Phase 1 advertising (which surrounds us, promoting conventional consumer products) cannot help sell something as specialized as hydraulic clutches, it most certainly is not true that this is the only capability of the IA&SP profession. As previously shown, advertising is only one of the seven tools.

The following specific tasks may be accomplished by employing any number or combination of the tools. The experienced practitioner faces his task without any hard-and-fast ideas as to what tools will be required. The selection, their final created form, the way they are used —all are dependent on the astute analysis of the sales problem and the jelling of the marketing strategy.

Tasks that IA&SP can help accomplish can be segregated into two categories: the kinds that might confront marketing planning and sales management, and the kinds that might confront salesmen in the field. Obviously, both are to a degree interrelated.

Tasks on Which IA&SP Can Assist Marketing Planning

- To make the product's existence, source, and buying benefits known to specific prospect audiences.
- To communicate vividly and quickly to all buying decision makers the product's use values.
- To attract interested responses from prospect account firms and individuals within such firms as a basis for a direct sales call.
- To save the time of field representatives by "preselling" so that face-to-face negotiations start at a point that much closer to the final purchase.
- To maintain interest in the company and the product for successive purchases of the same product or for purchases of other company products.
- To define market segments or identify additional potential markets.
- To create an image for the company or the product that will be conducive to closing a sale.
- To accelerate a changing technology that is to the advantage of the product being marketed.
- To distribute sales literature and promote prospects' sampling and trial, to develop contacts for demonstration.
- To discourage new competition from entering the field.
- To reach and influence top management decision makers not accessible to field representatives, and to do so without disrupting sales relations with lower echelon influentials.
- To exorcise "evil spirits"—that is, correct improper impressions, replace misinformation with facts.
- To build favorable personal reactions to the product, the company, and the company's policies and practices.
- To implant or accelerate adoption of a new technology, method, or trade practice favorable to the product or company.
- To establish a new end market or expand an end market for a product's primary customers.
- To educate, guide, and stimulate customers in the proper use of a product, thereby reducing and monitoring misuse.
- To open new markets or market segments or to broach secondary markets with minimum diversion of field sales efforts away from primary markets.
- To build a demand by the customers' customers for a construction material, an ingredient, or a component part in a fabricated or formulated end product.

- To create a special attendant service in relation to the product that either enhances its value or enlarges the company's role as a supplier.
- To multiply or expand a restricted use from an initial beachhead.
- To vividly and more convincingly communicate or demonstrate a use benefit or a product's performance.
- To champion a "cause" for an industry to win its member companies' favor as a preferred supplier.

Tasks on Which IA&SP Can Assist Field Selling

- To penetrate the account in maximum depth by creating a novel means of contact or a special reason for contact, or by providing an inducement to establish contact with all buying influentials.
- To favorably impress, build personal relations with, and influence "personalities" at key accounts.
- To build maximum pressure for a buying decision at a key account by providing the "packaged ammunition" for the critical call.
- To increase the percentage of actual sales in relation to "sales calls" by providing the most effective selling tools.
- To contribute materially to the effort to save a threatened account.
- To "unseat" competition at a specific account (or at a spectrum of accounts making up a market segment) by providing a helpful creative service, by devising a selling tool for customers, or by preparing a convincing presentation designed to show a product's strength or its competition's weakness.
- To presell accounts prior to a first contact by a field representative through providing sales tools for field men's local or regional use that are usable by the representative in his own operation planning.

In a sense, the foregoing listing constitutes a set of "skeletons," any of which can be transformed into a living, potent servant of sales by being fleshed with specific tools and marched in a timed program. But the calling to life requires the priceless stimulant of marketing management's designating the need, the task. That can only follow the analysis of the sales problem.

The "need" or "task" as defined and specified by company or marketing management is the sole foundation for building an IA&SP program.

In our dissection of the IA&SP discipline's capability, we can roughly classify programs into two categories. Depending on the marketing problems, either one or both kinds may be enlisted in the support of sales.

These are commonly short-range programs directed at a specific objective that may be a temporary impediment to sales progress. Task programs usually mark a transition from one to another of the three phases of the marketing evolution. They may span a few months or they may last as long as two years. They are created for the purpose of accomplishing a specified task within a specified period of time. A short-range program may require one or two, or any number of the seven sales tools. Some examples of short-range "tasks" and the tools they might use are as follows:

Task (Planning) To determine roughly the relative degree of interest in a new, low-cost sprinkler system by size and kind of plant as a starting point for market analysis.

Tools A media advertising program in two "horizontal" plant maintenance and management publications run for four months, couponed, offering sales literature.
A direct mail follow-up on all inquiries with a questionnaire coupled with an inducement to return the information that is sought.

Task (Field) To scotch the allegation that competition has made at 12 accounts in California that the company's specialty metal-cutting oil is flammable.

Tools Provide the field representative with a candle and a spray atomizer and a small kerosene-type lamp with a dozen new wicks. Program over a 30-day period a call at each customer to fill spray and lamp from the customer's inventory of product and demonstrate that liquid cannot be ignited as a fine mist or when wicked.

Task To build favor and a "preferred supplier" image in the cotton-dress manufacturing industry.

Tools Sponsor and partly or wholly finance a six-month media advertising program that publicizes the facts on the depressing effect on the industry of unrestricted imports. Create and produce a fact sheet on the industry's problem. Schedule the media program in suitable publications where the advertisements will be read by legislators. Provide industry customers with material for contacting their state and local representatives.

These are generally long-range programs whose purpose is to build an image for a company or a product, to provide a constant supply of leads for field follow-up, or for supplementing personal field call frequency with "mechanical" contacts to maintain a supplier position. If the objective is to build recognition for the company, to implant a vital idea so that it is inextricably connected with a specific product, or to establish respect for a particular capability—a long-range constant contact program is almost essential. A crash program can hardly serve. Three examples of constant contact programs are:

Objective   To plant firmly among chemical-processing-plant building and maintenance engineers the use-benefit fact that "our brand" of industrial-maintenance paint stops metal corrosion.

Program   Create a series of three ¼-page advertisements each, with the headline "Our Brand HALTS CORROSION" but with 50 to 60 words of factual body copy relating to acid exposure, alkaline exposure, and salt exposure. Run these advertisements three insertions per issue as 1, 2, 1; 2, 3, 2; 3, 1, 3, etc. in the two leading chemical processing publications steadily for two years.

Objective   To maintain and reinforce the image of the company as a highly capable fabricator of pressure vessels, storage tanks, and oil-refinery processing equipment.

Program   Create 11 jumbo-sized, 4-color postcards per year, each showing the completed job of a complicated and difficult construction fabricated to a demanding specification for a well-known processor. Explain the job in the postcard's legend. Mail a card monthly to a carefully maintained personalized list of 3,000 engineers concerned with specifying the supplier for processing-plant equipment.

The need for and values of constant contact advertising (highly pertinent when this tool is required by the company's marketing objectives) have been voluminously documented and reported in the literature. Tremendous amounts of research have been carried out by advertising agencies and media publishers as well as by market research firms, psychologists, and academicians. Since our concern is to explore the optimum way of making the most effective use of IA&SP we can leave the documentation of specific techniques to the experts. However, in our consideration of task and constant contact programs, one fact emerges: a task program is the more easily evaluated because its effects are usually tangible and reasonably immediate. Evaluation of a constant contact program, except for the type designed to provide a regular flow of sales leads, is more difficult. At this point, then, a few facts that justify the investment in constant contact advertising might be cited:

From Professor Hermann Ebbinghaus' findings, published in 1885, to the present time, all the evidence supports the premise that people forget a great deal very quickly. Ebbinghaus may have been the first to quantify the rate of forgetting, but the disheartening evidence is everywhere. Ebbinghaus' experiments showed both the value of repetition and the delicacy of implanted knowledge. Using a list of nonsense syllables, he found that one repetition of the list lodged 7 of the syllables in his memory, that 17 repetitions lodged 16 syllables, that 55 repetitions lodged 36. After an hour, he forgot about half; after six days, approximately 75 percent.

Aside from the need to combat "forgetting," there are other good reasons for maintaining frequency and continuity in constant contact advertising and promotion programs. One example: In a spot check on a first purchase of a "commodity chemical" from a major producer, it was found that 18 different individuals had had a voice in the selection of the supplier. One other: In a 1956 study of raw-materials purchasing practices involving 29 chemical processing companies, it was found that 63 percent of purchasing and sales management, 82 percent of production and engineering management, 70 percent of research and development management had a voice in the purchasing. Both of these findings indicate the importance of account penetration. Repetition guarantees wider reach, greater depth.

Another reason for constant contact advertising and promotion is that personnel changes are frequent. Commercial mailing list houses that maintain personal-name lists consider the lists obsolete in two years. Over a decade ago, McGraw-Hill published its study of 1,000 industrial buyers. The study showed that after one year only 435 list members had stayed in the same job, the same company, the same location. Thus the need for registering the message with new individuals in a changing audience over a period of time.

Then again, every industrial company has experienced self-initiated contacts from buyers, as well as orders that come in over the transom—where no salesman is involved. Such phenomena most often are the effect of the mechanized salesmanship of one or more of the selling tools the company has put in the field.

Constant contact advertising—in its lowest, most vapid form—too often has the flabby objective of simply "keeping our name (or product) before the public." But it can do much more than this.

Basically, constant contact advertising can be the sustained, reasonably frequent, year after year "selling" of a specific audience on products, services, or company by the implantation of strategic product knowledge, the dissemination of technological concepts, or the creation of an attractive image for a brand or company.

This, then, is the scope of marketing where IA&SP tools can serve. The next step is to examine how they are best put to work.

4

BUILDING
THE
FOUNDATION

Industrial companies can employ IA&SP for either or both of two major purposes. For our examination, we can consider them separately—although the two may overlap. To consider them separately, however, has a signal virtue: It permits us to distinguish between the two purposes on the basis of their objectives. And knowing the objective is the foundation for the creative thinking that builds the program, directs the selection and preparation of the tools that will be used, and organizes the way the program will run.

We have established that IA&SP is basically the craft of persuasive communication. The two purposes of such communication are selling the company and selling the product. Thus, we can establish one as corporate or institutional promotion, the other as product-selling promotion. The same seven kinds of tools are used for both, and the manner of planning is identical. Both require a solid foundation in the form of a specific objective—stated, clearly understood, and subscribed to by company, marketing, and promotion management. It is only upon this foundation that IA&SP can build programs and make its contribution to marketing and other aspects of the company's progress.

Let's examine both types of promotion.

CORPORATE PROMOTION

Many values are to be derived from promotion programs designed to sell the company. They range from the effect such a program can have as back-up for sales of the company products to the effect the program can have on the price-earnings ratio of the company's equities.

The size and the particular kind of program depend entirely on the objective, the audience(s), and the value to the company in communicating, registering, and sustaining the particular impression.

The objective for corporate advertising programs should be set by top management. The impression and reaction sought by this objective should be carefully weighed and should reflect both the company's present image needs and its longer-range needs. Corporate advertising should be in harmony with the needs of marketing; should have due regard to industrial, employee, and community relations; and should be conceived with an eye to future company growth. It must be recognized from the outset that a corporate image-building program is a long-range investment and must be planned accordingly.

As is the case with the task areas where IA&SP can help marketing, a catalog-style listing of all possible corporate objectives is impractical. Yet some of the key image-creating and communications tasks where IA&SP can serve the corporate interests can be outlined.

EVALUATION OF EQUITIES

It is a truism in the investment world that a common stock is worth what the buyer thinks it is worth. Present earnings and dividends are important, but often not so important as anticipated growth and earnings. Thus price-earnings ratios may range from 8 times to as much as 100 times present earnings. One of the factors that affect the equity evaluation of small to medium-size companies is knowledge of the company and its products or prospects. While many security analysts comb the lists, build financial dossiers, and search out detailed knowledge of companies, many other investors—including the private investor —do not. The initiative for supplying information to the financial community rests with the company. A corporate advertising program can and will call the attention of various security analysts, financial institutions, and private investors to a specific company. It will communicate information and create an image of the company that is important to the evaluation of its equities. If a company plans to go public or to raise additional capital, the equities of a known firm are easier to market than those of an unknown firm. Thus the discount required by an investment banker can be less if corporate advertising has made the firm and its products familiar to equity buyers.

A corporation—particularly a highly diversified one—can be a difficult thing to understand—and therefore an image that gets across its essence can be crucial. An advertisement is comprehensible; a corporation is not. If implanting knowledge of the company and its diversity is important to management, a corporate advertising program is the most practical way to communicate the essence of the company. The image built by the advertising is communicable, diversity or capability is reduced to an assimilable form, and the message reaches the audience considered important by the management.

Corporate advertising is an invaluable adjunct to the company's annual report, which reaches existing stockholders but cannot be circulated as broadly as company advertising. Where management wants the company's yearly performance to be broadly communicated, a corporate advertising program is the answer. Not only can it have a significant effect on the stock market's evaluation of the company's equities, but the image projected can be valuable in the kind of financing—common stock, preferred, convertibles, or debt—available to the company in the capital markets.

TECHNICAL COMPETENCE

In our competitive society, all industrial products require know-how. Certain types, such as machine tools, electronic process controls, material handling systems, and data processing equipment—particularly those products requiring a large capital investment—gain in buyer acceptability when the dimensions of the producer's technical capability are known. Thus a corporate advertising program that acquaints selected audiences with the company's in-depth knowledge of its field is a powerful marketing tool for a firm with a related but diversified product line. Such a program can be considered back-up for the product selling programs. Programs that register a convincing image of technical competence have a synergistic effect on product selling programs. The product selling programs themselves will have a more specific, narrower, and possibly a more oblique objective. Corporate advertising stressing technical competence can be a potent back-up, even if the product selling program does not employ media advertising.

In creating a "technical competence" program, it is important that the advertising truly register such competence, not merely talk about it. Technical competence is documented by successful installations, difficult problems solved, demanding customers satisfied, by citations, or by any other solid evidence of well-founded know-how. Bald statements or braggadocio—no matter how well worded—are not enough. The message must be convincing to the initiate of the particular technology referred to.

ATTRACTING PERSONNEL

Because of job changes, retirement, and death, an active, growing company requires a constant renewal of competent manpower. Yet the technical manpower pool of specialized engineers, administrators, researchers, production and sales managers has been relatively shallow for the past two decades. Thus, while the procurement of personnel of itself would rarely be a justifiable objective for a corporate advertising program, the incidental attraction of new employees is a definite value returned by such a program.

IMPROVED INDUSTRIAL, COMMUNITY, AND GOVERNMENT RELATIONS

A corporate advertising program or a special promotion program can be a valuable tool for making the company better accepted, for disclosing its policies, for stating its position on public issues, for making known its value to the community, and for explaining its internal employee practices. It can be a builder of prestige. The ends will determine the means; the objective will govern the creative approach, the tools used, and the timing and budget required. Of the numerous possible uses for corporate advertising, improving a particular set of external relations is most likely to develop as a task program rather than a constant contact program.

If it is valuable for a supplier of plant safety equipment to make itself better known in the automotive industry, a corporate program in those industrial publications serving the industry is warranted. The program will add stature to the company's safety helmets, protective clothing, sprinkler systems, and operations alarms—whose individual benefits can be promoted in product selling programs. If it is helpful in locating a new plant to have the goodwill of local officials and residents, a corporate advertising program can pave the way for construction sites, permits, local employment, and acceptance by residents. A corporate advertising program can explain the company's position and attitude on taxation, pending legislation, local regulations, and business practices.

These four broad areas where corporate promotion can serve particular company interests may be subdivided into dozens. Our major concern is to make the point that the communications need must be recognized by top management; the impression to be made or the image created must be specifically defined and the audiences designated.

Up to this point, corporate promotion does not ipso facto dictate media advertising. The program devised will depend on the objective and the analysis of the communication problem. This analysis and definition of the objective is as vital to "selling company" as it is to "selling product." It is the most essential step in IA&SP, providing the basic foundation for creating a program. Setting up this base is the practitioner's most important responsibility. Without it, neither corporate nor product promotion programs can attain their maximum effectiveness.

PRODUCT SELLING PROMOTION

"Marketing" analysis and sales planning are the most vital elements in the creation of effective IA&SP.

In the process of selling industrial products, there is a series of functional cells that make up the circuit designed to generate sales. We can diagram the circuit as shown in Exhibit 2.

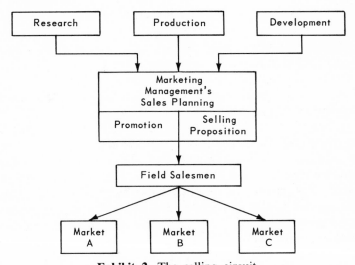

Exhibit 2. The selling circuit.

In the period between the early fifties and the mid-sixties, industrial goods manufacturers became conscious of the vast difference between "product selling" and "marketing." Fundamentally, product selling consisted of taking the product (and the "selling proposition" that presented it) indiscriminately to all potential users across a spectrum of industries and securing orders. The product and its selling proposition were developed in the form of a common denominator that would have a median, across-the-board appeal for all. Sales management consisted primarily of setting quotas and fielding and motivating salesmen to meet them. The R&D effort aimed at minimizing complaints and improving the product where possible. New-product R&D often had no interface with marketing.

The product selling system, however, offered no insurance against product obsolescence. Industrial needs, advancing technologies, and operating methods were changing rapidly. It is obvious that the finest quality, lowest cost, hand-operated circuit breaker could not be sold by triple the sales force when automatic, self-actuating circuit breakers were made available. This was both a competitive and a technological force. There were also technological forces—as there were when, to take a basic example, the advent of the motor car all but wiped out the buggy whip, the horseshoeing, and the anvil industries. It became apparent that to thrive—or even survive—a business would be better advised to "serve markets" than to simply "sell product." This new posture was termed "market orientation." Today, the business-literature shelves bulge with treatises and periodicals on the subject.

Fundamentally, the marketing management of today is best advised to concentrate on *markets*. A market is defined as a group of potential customers who buy the product for the same use. Business semantics have refined this to "market segments," but for our purposes we can use the simpler term "markets," as illustrated by the following hypothetical example.

The ABC Company makes forklift trucks. These are useful to printers, who move reams of paper; to frozen food companies that load cases in refrigerated transport; to soap companies that move packed products around warehouses. These three industries would represent three different markets. To be market-oriented, the ABC Company would make its forklift truck (and devise its selling proposition) so that it best fitted the needs of *each* of these markets. This might entail product modification that involved height of lifting, weight handled per load, materials of construction, speed, and design of lifting platform. Equally important, it might involve the selling proposition.

For example, an astute marketing manager analyzing the frozen-food-handling market might determine that profit margins were small and that the changing seasonal pack-outs varied greatly in weight and bulk. Based on these market facts, he might develop for the frozen food market a selling proposition such as the following oriented to these special needs of this particular market.

The ABC Company would develop a series of four attachment lifting grapplers that would handle perfectly the range of sizes required by the different seasonal pack-outs. They would *sell* these grapplers to the frozen food companies. The lifts to operate the grapplers would be *leased* to the customers for a period of five years, then reconditioned and sold into another market. A selling proposition of this type would both conserve the capital of this particular market and provide the market with a machine exactly suited to its needs. But most important, this analysis of the market's needs would provide marketing planning with knowledge of the market, its size, the competitive forces, the major target customers, and the trade practices. The market analysis enables marketing planning to assess the market potential, to set a sales goal in the market, and to marshal the forces of field selling and promotion for the task of achieving that goal.

In short, marketing orientation consists of meeting the market's needs—with the product and with the selling proposition. While tailoring the product is a responsibility of R&D, the input of IA&SP can be a critical factor in the selling proposition. In certain special instances, the promotion itself can constitute the selling proposition.

From market knowledge comes the basis for the creation of the marketing mix. From the IA&SP practitioner's standpoint, marketing management need take but one additional critically important analytical step: determine the pressure point in the particular market.

> The *"pressure point"* is WHO must be made to do WHAT to induce the potential customers making up the market to buy the product.

The marketing objective and the specific definition of the pressure point are the entire foundation for the creation of the promotion program. They set the parameters for the tools to be used, provide the guide for creating the tools that *are* required, indicate the timing and logistics of the program, and justify the expenditure of the promotional budget.

The final responsibility for defining the pressure point is an obligation of marketing management, although the IA&SP practitioner and market research may collaborate. But it is important to stress that

> The definition of the pressure point is so vital to the effectiveness of an IA&SP program that the responsibility for defining it must rest with the marketing individual responsible for marketing success.

If the pressure point is *incorrect,* the created program will not attain its maximum effectiveness or may even fail completely. If the stated pressure point is vague, generalized, or diffuse, it may be impossible to create a program designed to stimulate the nonspecific action sought. If the pressure point is not the most significant one, the promotion-program investment will not net the highest possible return.

The pressure point is the starting point for the entire creative process that is the responsibility of the IA&SP practitioner—be he an account man in an agency or the promotion manager within the company.

It is in this area of the industrial marketing art that so much promotion goes awry, that so much remains undone. Conversely, it is detailed market knowledge, realistic marketing objectives, and clearly defined pressure points that underpin the many excellent IA&SP programs that can be found in the various trades. Relatively speaking, the creative component of a promotion program is less important than the program's orientation with respect to the marketing objectives, indeed far less critical than the specificity and correctness of the pressure point defined. Superb creativity in the advertising, the literature, and the other "tools" will not make a program effective unless it is solidly based on sound marketing analysis and planning. In fact, indifferent or even substandard creativity in the "tools" may detract only a little from the effectiveness of a solidly based program.

We can now tie together the components that cumulatively form the input for effective IA&SP programs.

1.   Marketing management's thorough knowledge of the anatomy of the market—shared with the promotion practitioner.

2.   Marketing management's setting of a specific objective, a sales goal in the market over a definite period of time—made clear to the promotion practitioner.

3.   Marketing management's definition of the "pressure point" (*who* must be made to do *what*) in the market audience so that the objective is achieved—written out as carefully as a treaty clause for the promotion practitioner.

4.   The IA&SP practitioner's creation of a timed program to help secure the action specified by the pressure point, and presented for marketing management's approval.

Every agency account man and every industrial promotion manager will agree that components 1, 2, and 3 are the most essential inputs in the circuit. Without them, creativity flaps in the wind and there is no foundation upon which to build a promotion program. Lacking this fundamental information, the marketing executive himself cannot determine if, where, and how a promotion program can help him reach his sales goal; he cannot judge the validity, aptness, and potential effectiveness of a proposed program; he cannot assess the prudence of the promotion investment required for the program.

The IA&SP practitioner's job responsibility is to create and operate effective promotional programs. His training, his experience, and his ability should fit him to produce every one of the seven types of tools of persuasive communication. It is obvious, however, that a stonemason cannot begin to build the walls for a house without dimensions and a plan. But industry is rife with promotion structures for which the promotion builder either has been given no plan or has had only a glance at an incomplete drawing.

In industrial marketing, the relatively lower value that is placed on promotion as compared to consumer product marketing is reflected in the financing of the marketing mix. In consumer packaged goods, the percent of gross sales spent on promotion may range from 10 to 40 percent. Advertising and promotion carry the major burden of moving the product. In major appliances, it may range from 5 to 15 percent. In this area, promotion is assisted by retail salesmen. In industrial products, the average is in the neighborhood of 0.75 to 1 percent—an indication that promotion is relegated to a very minor role.

Our purpose in detailing the complex and essential base for effective promotion is to point out that its improper use or underemployment is traceable more to myopic marketing planning than to any deficiency of the discipline itself.

5

HOW THE ENDS DETERMINE THE MEANS

To illustrate the importance of the marketing management's three inputs—market anatomy, marketing objective, and pressure point—to the creation and the effectiveness of IA&SP promotion programs, let us consider the effect of variants on the following hypothetical examples. The three inputs from marketing govern IA&SP's application of every concept thus far defined. They define the promotion practitioner's creative planning problem; they determine his selection of tools; they are a basis for the creative "thinkout" and production of the program tools; and, finally, they govern the budget, the timing, and the logistics.

Factors and forces in the market's anatomy reverberate through the entire creative process of developing a potent promotion program. A clear understanding of this fact of life is essential for the creation of viable programs.

ANATOMY OF THE MARKET

In determining the anatomy of the market, you must have more than statistical data. Numbers are not enough! The size (in units or dollars) and a numerical summary of potential customers represent the *starting* point. In addition, you must have a knowledge of the market's purchasing practices and the concentration of buying potentials, a familiarity with the competition's strengths and weaknesses, and an understanding of pricing and trade practices as well as technological trends and operating procedures. This detailed analysis of the market becomes the basis for setting the marketing objective. It must be sufficiently detailed to determine the all-important pressure point.

MARKETING OBJECTIVE

In setting the sales or marketing objective, it is not enough to have a "percent increase" or a sales goal in dollars. The objective should be stated in terms of the desired market share, the number of new accounts to be added, the increase in business sought from existing accounts, or the number of units to be sold. The marketing goals should be defined in terms of "quantity" and "time." And the objective should determine the general plan of how this is to be done. Setting the marketing objective can only be done by someone who knows the market, who in the light of this knowledge sets a realistic but optimistic goal, and who formulates a sales plan by which the goal can be achieved.

The final marketing plan should, in a sense, be left open to admit the IA&SP input. Aside from pricing, territories, major account plans, salesmen action, and so on, the IA&SP function's creative contribution can affect all the conventional selling forces. It can be a vital part of the selling proposition. This input, however, cannot be created until the pressure point is clearly defined.

PRESSURE POINT

In every marketing problem there may appear to be dozens of pressure points—and indeed there are. However, only one or two, or at most three, are critical. It is the task of knowledgeable marketing management to determine them. Take the following examples.

As his marketing goal, a formulator of Brand X wood preservatives wants at least half of all the poles and structural lumber used over the next two years in official road signs and highway guards in his state to be treated with his wood preservative. In analyzing "who must be made to do what" marketing management might come up with a single, all-encompassing idea as the pressure point: "The state legislature must be made to pass a law that all highway construction lumber must be treated with Brand X." Unquestionably, this is a most critical pressure point. However, the probability of its being achieved in two years—or ever—is very low indeed. The very improbability invalidates this as a reasonable pressure point. It is the prerogative of the experienced IA&SP practitioner to judge the practicality of a pressure point. When it is too general, too grandiose, or too unreasonable, the marketer must try again to find a practical strategy.

An IA&SP program is created to work on *people*. It is essential to know who are the most influential individuals, what echelons of management are most important, or what job stratums most influence the buying decision.

The pressure point should particularize the most important influentials. These people may be in a given echelon across an industry or in a particular function of a given market. For the purposes of creating effective promotion programs, it does not matter if the "who" is 50 individuals in 10 companies, 1,000 individuals in 200 companies, or 100,000 individuals in any number of companies. The number involved affects only the selection of tools. What is important is that the "who" should indeed be the most highly influential and that the specific way the group is to be made to think and act will indeed have the desired effect in the marketing program. In brief, the pressure point must be sound and reasonable. It must be simple and specific. It is possible that a single marketing problem may have two or even three pressure points. If this is the case, each will require an individually designed promotion program. However, in any one marketing problem, most frequently one pressure point will predominate as the factor affecting a significant success.

Our purpose in this section is to demonstrate how important it is to know the market, to set the marketing objective, and to define the significant pressure point. We will do this by showing the effect on a promotion program of variants in a deliberately simplified, hypothetical marketing problem.

The ABC Company is one of three manufacturers of forklift trucks. It is smaller than Hi-Lift Co., larger than Easy-Move, Inc. Forklift trucks are used throughout industry. Up to this point in time, all three companies had offered a range of models differing primarily in size and power. Forklifts were sold across all types of industry. All three companies advertised in *Business Week* and *Materials Handling* magazines. Catalogs were used to answer inquiries, and field salesmen followed them up by call, phone, or letter.

The ABC Company made an overall study of the use of forklifts in industry, and segregated seven distinct markets. One of these was the printers' market.

A close study showed that there were 19,000 printing plants in the U.S.; that 7,000 of these used from two to five forklifts to handle paper; that 3,500 used five to fifteen; that 500 used fifteen or more. In the large printing plants, the choice of capital equipment was handled by either the general manager or the production superintendent. In small plants, equipment was purchased by the owners. The lift operators were minimum-wage laborers. Reams of paper were often badly damaged by poor lift handling, and expensive and bulky wood pallets were used to minimize such damage. The average large printing plant replaced its lifts every five years; the smaller plants used them indefinitely. Over half the lifts in use were Hi-Lift models; ABC and Easy-Move shared the balance.

CASE 1

Assume that this anatomy of the market is accurate and includes all significant information. The ABC marketing planner sees immediately that he has a Phase 2 problem: to improve his position over that of competition. He then sets forth his goal.

Marketing objective: To sell ABC lifts to the 3,500 largest printers as replacements for Hi-Lifts, with a target of having at least two ABC's in every large plant in five years and 50 percent of the plants completely converted to ABC's by that time.

Pressure point: The general managers and production superintendents of the 3,500 largest printing plants must be induced to evaluate the performance of ABC's in their plants.

PROMOTION PROGRAM BUILT ON THIS PRESSURE POINT

Tool A. A 24″ by 36″ flip-over presentation that shows the "Flat-Guard" lifter of the ABC that is designed so it does not injure paper packages. This presentation is prepared for a direct sales call on six of the largest printers. It offers a 50 percent discount on one ABC lift in return for a three-month performance evaluation in the printing plant and permission to use the printer's name and data in promotion. The objective is to get three significant case histories from six target calls.

Tool B. A basic sales brochure illustrated with paper-handling close-ups that "sells" the savings in paper spoilage with ABC handling.

Tool C. As a start, a three-advertisement campaign run four times each in *Printer & Lithographer* magazine, each ad citing one of the secured case histories with the headlines beamed at management; for example:

SURREY PRESS MANAGEMENT SAYS:
"ABC LIFTS SAVED US $1,100 PAPER
SPOILAGE IN 90 DAYS"

WILLIS' PRINTING CO.'S SUPERINTENDENT
FINDS ABC LIFTS END SHORT-FALL RUNS
DUE TO PAPER DAMAGE.

"ABC LIFTS ARE SAVING US A REAM OF
PAPER IN EVERY CARLOAD," REPORTS
HUNTINGTON LITHOGRAPHY.

Tool D. A first-class, personal-letter, direct-mail campaign carrying reprints of the ads sent to the general managers of the 500 largest printing plants requesting the opportunity to demonstrate the equipment. Three different letters sent over four months, dropping plants from the list as direct field contacts are established.

After four months, the three ads are mailed successively with a printed tip-on three weeks apart to the remaining 3,000 large plants.

Tool E. Provide all 12 field salesmen with photographs of paper package damage from Hi-Lifts and a six-inch section of the ABC's polished knife-edge lift.

CASE 2

With the market anatomy as before, assume that a *different* marketing objective has been set.

Marketing objective: To obtain in-the-plant trial use of at least 5 ABC lifts in 100 of the 500 largest printing plants over the next 2 years.

Pressure point: The general managers of 100 out of the 500 largest printing plants must be induced to make trial use of at least 5 ABC lifts over the next 24 months.

PROMOTION PROGRAM BUILT ON THIS PRESSURE POINT

Tool A. A 20-minute moving picture produced to show typical damage to paper packages by forklift handling, with scenes that dramatize short-fall runs, small lot reorders, excess washups to finish runs, and so forth. This is pictorially contrasted with the performance of ABC lifts with close-ups showing the way an ABC works to protect paper packages.

Tool B. A 24″ x 36″ flip-over "costs saved" presentation that shows graphically the costs of damaged paper, time lost, fill-in runs for short falls, and so forth over a year's time. Ends with offer of a 90-day free trial of five machines.

Tool C. Printed invitation cards for local use by the field representatives inviting a general manager and his production superintendent to a luncheon or dinner meeting. These invitations are designed to be personalized and dated by local field men. For each local meeting arranged, a minimum of three printing firms and a maximum of five will be called together for a showing of the film followed by the "costs saved" presentation.

Tool D. A personal letter from the president of the ABC Company timed and sent to successive groupings of 15 general managers of printing plants in each local area. The letter points out the hidden drain on operating profits and advises that this will be documented by the local field man. Copies of these letters go to the field representative, who follows up with the invitation and holds the meetings.

Tool E. A basic sales brochure illustrated with paper-handling close-ups that "sells" the savings in paper spoilage with ABC handling.

CASE 3

Assume an additional factor in the market. For example, assume that in the thorough study of the printers' market it was learned that a significant technological trend was starting. In an effort to reduce paper-handling damage, two of the major paper producers were developing disposable, corner- and edge-protecting kraft pallets—a system radically different from the current, made-on-the-spot wood pallets. ABC could see that other paper producers would follow suit and that producer palletizing would soon be standard. A modification of the standard ABC model—though unpatentable—would dovetail perfectly with the new pallet. (ABC R&D is asked to work closely with the two paper companies to make certain the ABC lift has the maximum efficiency.)

Marketing objective: To induce each of the 25 major paper producers to recommend ABC lifts to their printing-plant customers as they convert to disposable pallets.

Pressure point: The marketing management of the 25 major printing paper producers must be induced to recommend ABC lifts to their printer customers.

Tool A. Slide presentation in filmstrip form for desk or large meeting showing made up to demonstrate how the ABC lift works with the new protective pallet. This presentation is designed to show the efficiency of the ABC lift. Showings are programmed so that the presentation is shown successively to the marketing management of the paper companies and their paper salesmen. Copies of the presentation are made available in printed form to the paper companies for passing on to their printer customers.

Tool B. A sales brochure written and designed to show the advantages of the paper makers' new protective disposable pallet and the procedure for handling paper packages with the ABC lift. This brochure is designed so that it can be imprinted by the paper producer and in turn given to his printer customers when he converts his paper stocks to the new pallet.

These examples show how the ends determine the means. The marketing objective and the pressure point are the determinants of the tools, the promotion program's conception and logic, and the justification for its budget.

The foregoing hypothetical marketing problem illustrates the three basic concepts that are the sine qua non of effective industrial promotion.

1. Thorough knowledge of the market. This is essential to select the marketing objective, to formulate the marketing plan, and to define the pressure point on which the sales-assisting promotion program must be built.

2. A specific objective and a general marketing plan to attain it. This is the precursor to specifying the pressure point.

3. The pressure point. This is the foundation for the creative planning upon which the promotion program is built.

The pressure point specifies who must be made to do what. The IA&SP program provides the tools to communicate "why." In essence, the program packages up the sales proposition in its clearest, most succinct, most persuasive form. In special instances, the IA&SP program itself can be the sales proposition. In marketing undifferentiated commodities this can often occur: A commodity supplier mounts a promotion program that is entirely in the interest of a given customer market. When the salesmen show this effort made in behalf of the customer's market, it is easy to prove that the company deserves a share (for a new account) or a greater share (with existing accounts) of the buyer's requirements of the commodity.

The handling of these three concepts of industrial marketing and promotion planning will make or break a manufacturer's investment in promotion. They are unique to industrial marketing. Though the problems have many interrelated factors, there is little commonality between companies for establishing guidance precedents. Fewer outside services are available, and in a diversified company the planning and promotion man-hours available "per market" are usually far fewer than they are with consumer products. On balance, the industrial marketing planner's task is far more complex than that of his counterpart in consumer products. Conversely, the industrial promotion practitioner's task—once his base has been provided—is less demanding, since the more or less intuitive creativity so essential to successful consumer-product promotion is far less of a factor in industrial selling.

In summary, the key to successful IA&SP programs is marketing analysis, planning, and the definition of pressure points. The ends determine the means. The creative task after the ends are specified is primarily applying logic and competence in the building of the tools.

6

CREATING
SOLID
PROGRAMS

An IA&SP program is an idea, a concept translated into concrete tools. It is also the tactics for putting the tools to work. The creation of a program grows basically from knowing what has to be communicated to whom, from recognizing clearly the impression it must make and the action sought, and from conceiving the kinds of tools that will be needed to do the job. The program as a whole is an instrument to inform, convince, and persuade in such a way as to stimulate the desired action. There is no limit to the variety in content or format and the manner of field use of the seven types of promotional tools. No formula can prescribe particular combinations of tools for a given promotional task.

The creation of a promotion program depends on the expertise of the practitioner; his must be the choice of tools. The viability of the program as a whole, therefore, and the quality of the tools he creates are in direct proportion to his competence. There is no substitute for a solid foundation. Ornamentation will not disguise shaky marketing underpinning, nor will heavy financing replace a missing or badly targeted pressure point.

Basic to the conception of an IA&SP program is the product's "selling proposition." The most primitive selling proposition is the product in a utility package that protects it during shipment and a price list that gives the product's bare specifications, cost, and terms of payment. From this level, the selling proposition can expand into incredibly complex forms.

Basically, the selling proposition is dressing up the offering for purchase in such a manner as to make buying attractive, easy, and hard to resist. The promotion program can be an integral part of the selling proposition; indeed in some unusual marketing problems the promotion program *is* the selling proposition. Thus in devising the selling proposition it is to the marketing planner's advantage to have the input of his promotion practitioner if for no other reason than that the latter can present the selling proposition in its most communicable form. But more often, the promotion practitioner can contribute creative ideas. At the least, the promotion man will have a grass-roots knowledge of the selling proposition to guide him in his creation of the program's selling tools. The collaboration of the marketing-planning manager and the promotion manager in detailing the selling proposition is frequently as synergistically fruitful as the mutual creativity of an agency copywriter and an art director in the conception of an advertisement.

Industrial marketers on the average are less sophisticated in the creation of selling propositions than the marketers of consumer products. Consumer product companies burgeon with attractive selling propositions, ranging from tire companies' "no money down" to record makers' "stereo player for $19.95 (records $4.50)." One reason many industrial firms tend to neglect the selling proposition is that technical products are bought more for considerations of reason, price, and performance than because of emotion, impulse, or habit. Nevertheless, innovation in devising the selling proposition can have a significant effect in marketing success with industrial products. Well-known examples include leased rather than sold computers, specially matched material-handling systems between producer and user, consigned stocks, and special services offered, such as architectural layout services for prefabricated buildings. To these can be added a number of strictly promotional services, such as printed or audiovisual training courses for your customers' personnel, the establishment and promulgation of a "standard of quality" by which your customers' products are distinguished from their competition's, the providing of ancillary hand tools, measuring devices, testing kits, instructional markings, and reuse containers—benefits, in short, that are not available from the competition. IA&SP creativity can sweeten the basic sales proposition.

In marketing, the supplier who is most successful is the one who best satisfies the customer's needs. These needs may range across the price and performance of the product, its in-plant handling efficiency, the customer's own product marketing needs, and influential individuals' personal and professional needs.

Industrial marketing must then be viewed as a need-satisfying relationship in which both the supplier and the buyer obtain the maximum satisfaction and profit. The more ancillary need satisfactions that can be built into the selling proposition, the more attractive it becomes for the buyer.

Devising ancillary need satisfactions for the selling proposition is a creative task. In the marketing of safety goggles, there may be no reason why the packing case cannot be a portable "storage cabinet" and the individual goggle box a slip-in compartment. In marketing electrical wire or metal strapping for kraft shipping cases, it may be helpful to the user if you have an imprinted "graduation" showing the amount in lineal feet still left on the spool. In marketing clay plant pots to commercial greenhouses, it can be highly beneficial if the shipping cases are so designed as to be easily made into convenient holders for the plants the grower ultimately sells.

Ancillary benefits in the selling proposition can be of enormous value in the marketing of undistinguished or commodity-type products. In some instances, a promotion program can be the *entire* selling proposition—as in the following hypothetical example:

A manufacturer offers a basic, commodity germicide for use in formulating germ-controlling floor waxes for hospitals. To make his selling proposition more attractive than the competition's, the manufacturer institutes a comprehensive and objective testing program that proves the effectiveness of floor wax formulations containing a specific concentration level of his material. Thereafter, he creates and legally protects a distinguishing label marking, advertises to hospital administrators the effectiveness of products so marked, and offers the use of the distinguishing marking to buyers of his commodity germicide.

A selling proposition can be made more appealing in an almost limitless variety of ways. It can range from a problem-solving service to training for customers' personnel. It can take the form whereby a component supplier (such as an electric-motor producer) furnishes a warranty on his product for a customer market, such as food-mixer manufacturers, to merchandise. A supplier of rodent-control compounds can provide "ready-to-use, packaged promotions" to professional-exterminator customers for their own local or regional use. The only general guidelines a marketing or promotion planner can set for himself for devising and judging the appeal and innovation value of a selling proposition are two.

1. Has the same selling proposition or method of communicating it been used before in the customer market? (If so, it may be an innovation for the company—but not for the customer market.)

2. How forceful an appeal does it have when viewed from the customer-market's standpoint. (Put yourself in the prospect's shoes and ask: "What does this mean to me?" If there isn't a solid answer, the selling proposition is weak.)

To devise an attractive selling proposition, knowledge of market needs, a realistic appraisal of the product's cost and performance, and an evaluation of competition are essential. On this foundation, marketing and promotion can create the most appealing selling proposition. It can be as simple as providing the complete technical information, use benefits, and purchase costs in the most communicable, easy-to-comprehend form. It can be as sophisticated as a special method of payment, an ancillary technical service, or a help-the-customer market-promotion program. Sometimes the packaging of the selling proposition in its most convincing form can be as important as the proposition itself. In devising a selling proposition, the promotion practitioner can be a useful contributor.

THE CREATION OF PROGRAMS

Creativity is the hallmark of IA&SP, but it can be stultified in a number of ways. It is most often thwarted in a company oriented to product selling. Since the product-selling posture is basically short-range, month-by-month securing of orders by a hard-driving sales force, promotion is held to a minimum. In such an environment, the marketing planning is minimal and the use of promotion in specific marketing tasks and for long-range company values may be ignored. One tool, however, is invariably demanded: product literature.

Creative capability can be diluted to the point of less than significant usefulness when the in-house manpower (or agency-supplied service) is spread tissue-thin over a variety of products in a multiplicity of markets. And the creative capability will be completely short-circuited unless the marketing planning function analyzes the anatomy of a market, decides on a specific marketing objective, and astutely determines the pressure point.

The pressure point is the basis for creating a program. It is the stimulant for the creative process, the specification for the communications task, the compass for the program's course, and the determinant of the required tools. As in scientific research, the definition of the problem is all-important before work can begin. In IA&SP, the same applies. The pressure point is the statement of the problem.

For any given pressure point, there may be several possible programs involving differing combinations of tools. However, programs that are professionally recommended should be accepted and run as a package. A competent promotion practitioner can provide more than one approach to solving a communications problem. Yet pieces of differing programs patched together rarely work. Integrated programs can be created with "price tags." They should be accepted on the basis of their creative viability, their probability of success, and the value that will be received from the costs. Programs that are emasculated for budget reasons may be totally ineffective, or, more often, worth far less than alternative programs made up with a reasonable cost ceiling in view from the outset. When the coat is made to fit the cloth, it is well to have a general idea of the amount of cloth before the styling is attempted. As will be covered in a later section, the budget for promotion must be viewed as an investment in the light of the task it is designed to accomplish.

Creativity is required in both the conception of the program and the building of the tools. The latter step begins once the program strategy is conceived, approved, and budgeted. While no hard-and-fast rules can be set up for creating the tools, some guidelines can be established.

Aptness. A program for which the pressure point is top management will obviously differ greatly in physical appearance, tone, and benefits promised from a program directed at purchasing agents or design engineers. A program selling an expensive piece of capital equipment or a critical technical service will require an image vastly different from that of a program selling a production-line stapling system or an industrial maintenance paint. This sensitivity to the aptness of the copy tone and content and the graphic appearance of the advertisements and literature is intuitive and conditioned. It is transgressed most often by graphic artists or copywriters who have little or no real feeling for the business or who are rigid in their approach. In industrial communications in general, any resort to bizarre styling or "clever" copy is self-defeating. Clear, succinct, factual, and complete copy and clean, attractive graphics will invariably prove most effective.

Consistency. Every appearance of media advertising and every exposure of a prospect audience to one or more of the communication tools should be considered a "message" that impacts the "who" of the pressure point. Obviously, the message will be more emphatic if a basic consistency of both content and appearance is maintained. A basic theme should therefore be used to reinforce the message, and this should be repeated in all the tools of the program to increase its conviction and memorability. In building the tools, it is important to see that the message that condenses the selling proposition is maintained consistently in every phase of the program. Similarly, a harmony of graphics should be maintained in all the program tools.

Exploitation. During the course of a program, there will be primary effects from the appearance of the advertising in various publications, the returns from mailings, and the traffic at trade shows and exhibits. The astute practitioner, however, should be acutely aware of the secondary values of his communications and exploit them accordingly. Among the many ways of so proceeding, the following are the most obvious.

Provide all field men with a supply of preprints of the advertisements. Since these advertisements graphically condense the selling proposition into its most communicative form, they make helpful conversation pieces for field work and lend graphic stature to the product discussed. The majority of industrial products cannot be carried as samples by salesmen. Advertisements make visual substitutes. Preprints can also be mailed as the attachment to a direct mail sales letter. The *fact* of the advertising can be the reason for the mailing.

Take detailed pictures of trade exhibits. A picture story of an exhibit in the hands of a field salesman can recall the exhibit and its message to prospects who saw it; it can bring the exhibit and its message to those who did not attend.

Build a salesman's handout and a direct mail piece from a series of advertisements, thereby making the printed piece into a convincing story of the product benefits. The campaign itself can be fleshed with additional copy on the number of satisfied customers, specific user testimonials, lists of prestige-building buyers, or other evidences of acceptance. Promotional pieces of this nature have a high degree of assurance value, making a prospect feel more comfortable in reaching a buying decision.

TIMING AND COORDINATION

An IA&SP program can be strengthened or weakened by the scheduling. A program must be viewed as a total communication impact on a particular audience over a specific period of time. The tools selected, their deployment, and their interaction with field work must all be coordinated for maximum effect. This timing begins with the creation of the tools themselves.

After "selling" a program to management, the practitioner will do well to stipulate a sufficiently long lead time for the building of the program's tools and thereafter the time to inform, educate, and enlist the cooperation of the field force in every aspect of the program's workings and its follow-up.

In creating the program's sales tools, collateral material such as literature, salesmen's samples or demonstration aids, target-account sales presentations, moving pictures, and so forth require a far longer time to produce than the media advertising. Therefore, work on these tools should begin first. Finished art for media advertisements might well be postponed until cleared manuscripts and layouts are on hand for all collateral material. Above all, media advertising that requires literature, visual aids, or field demonstration kits should not appear until all the follow-up material is at hand. A program that is conceived as a package will operate most effectively that way. It is bound to suffer if it is fielded piecemeal or in poor order. Never let an advertisement appear without having on hand, ready to go, all the material needed to handle the response that the advertisement is likely to generate, and never let it appear before the field salesmen are fully informed and prepared. If media advertising is not part of the program, the principle of coordination in using the tools still holds true.

In industrial promotion, the practitioners can be roughly divided into "creative" and "administrative" individuals or departments. The creative practitioners are those who themselves do the maximum amount of writing and production. The practitioners working in administration are those who obtain the creative work from advertising agencies or outside services. All the tools of promotion start from a blank sheet of paper. The most common practice is for industrial firms to prepare all the collateral materials themselves and rely on their advertising agency for the media advertising tool. In small firms, the entire job may be handled by the agency; in very large firms, all creative work may be done inside and the agency used simply for production and traffic. This last practice is unusual, since creating media advertising is a demanding calling best left in the hands of specialists. Whatever the modus operandi, the principles for creating effective promotion must still be observed. Close rapport with a capable agency is essential for the contribution such an agency can make to the media advertising and to the program as a whole.

THE MEDIA ADVERTISING TOOL

In IA&SP, the advertising component is usually the most costly component of a program. As is the case with trade exhibits and moving pictures, the services of specialists are essential. But the industrial practitioner cannot expect an outside specialist to work from nothing. The excellence of an advertising campaign, a trade exhibit, or a moving picture is usually in direct proportion to the amount and quality of the information and guidance provided the specialists. In the case of media programs, the agency should be privy to the anatomy of the market, the marketing objective, the pressure point, and the conception of the program as a whole. With this as its base, the creative vitality of the media advertising will be in direct proportion to the agency's capability.

The following criteria for judging media advertising were set forth by Irving Lanning, of the Gardner Advertising Agency, many years ago. The writer has found no other system so simple and complete for analyzing the viability of an advertising program at the copy and layout stage. If the advertisement does not stand up on all three counts, the Lanning method makes it possible to identify the area of weakness rather than simply saying, "I don't like the ad," or "Somehow, this ad just doesn't do the job." The three criteria follow.

1. *How well does it carry out the* basic strategy *of the marketing campaign?* This relates to the marketing plan. It is the selection of the strongest selling appeal of the product for the particular prospect audience in the particular market. It is in effect the selling proposition on which the advertisement must be based, and only this will determine how much impact the message can have on the reader. Under this criterion, it is essential to evaluate exactly how the advertisement matches the pressure point's "who (for copy, tone, and appeal) must be made to do what (for action spur)."

2. *How strong is the* selling creativity *of the message?* This is a measure of how well the advertising sells or convinces the reader. It is a test of the skill with which the selling proposition is presented or the product's strongest selling points are converted into convincing words and pictures.

3. *How effective is the* surface creativity *of the message?* This is the graphic power of the message to call attention to itself, to capture the reader's interest with the vitality and originality of its appearance. It is the combined power of selling and surface creativity that stops and sells the reader and determines how effectively the advertisement will do its job.

In industrial advertising surface creativity, of itself, can never be enough. The most unusual attention-getting power or the most clever or bizarre graphics are no substitute for proper orientation to the marketing plan and technically impressive, convincingly presented, and need-related buying benefits. It is the substitution of electrifying but superficial surface creativity for a market strategy and an underlying solid objective that most often produces industrial advertising of little value to the advertiser. Conversely, a correctly determined pressure point and a forceful message brought to bear can do much to make a rather pedestrian-looking advertisement surprisingly effective. It is essential to remember that industrial-buying influentials read to get information and to serve logical self-interests. Thus there is far less need to grab attention and practically no need to reach for emotional effect.

7
ESTABLISHING A BUDGET

The practices used in establishing promotional budgets run the gamut from the sublime to the ridiculous. One company makes it a practice to set a percentage of the previous year's sales as an allocation for the succeeding year's promotion. (For promotion-sensitive products, this method can only mean built-in cyclic death, or profitless prosperity.) Another arbitrarily sets a ceiling figure that covers five product groups, and the marketing and promotion managers must vie for a portion of the available funds. Still another develops a total selling-expense budget with the recommended aggregate promotion costs at the bottom of the list. If the total selling expenses are too high the reductions are made in the promotion sector. Still another keeps close tabs on what the competition is doing, obtaining its data from published measured media and collateral estimates, and sets its budgets accordingly. The most logical and common-sense method is the one that is the most rarely used—and then only by highly sophisticated companies. That method is simply the "task" method.

Anomalies in setting promotion budgets stem from top management's or marketing management's mistaken or incomplete understanding of what IA&SP is and what it can do. Excessive budgets and spendthrift, pointless programs (which usually are short-lived) are rooted in a mystical belief that promotion is magic and can work miracles. Niggardly budgets and substandard programs result from management's not comprehending that promotion is simply another force in the marketing mix, that it can and should be used to carry out a specialized, often essential part of the marketing program. IA&SP is neither a miracle worker nor a sterile cost of doing business. Because industrial management is surrounded by consumer advertising, because it recognizes the vast differences between consumer marketing and its own technical products and marketing problems, it tends to lump all "advertising" together and discount its value in industrial selling. A prime responsibility of the agencies and practitioners is to correct such mistaken impressions. This can be done by the application of the methods and planning principles we have been examining and by the task method of budgeting promotion. The value of IA&SP programs is simply assessed; it relates to the worth of the task they carry out in the marketing program.

The task method is integral to marketing planning. It is based on the value of achieving the marketing objective. It is dependent on a realistic appraisal of the marketing task and the means for accomplishing it. IA&SP designates and accepts that part of the selling task it can handle less expensively or more effectively than anyone else. It sets the minimum budget for a specific, integrated program designed for a particular communication (and persuasion) job.

There are a variety of ways of gauging the prudence of investment in advertising and promotion. The method to be used depends, however, on the particular marketing problem and the value returned by the marketing plan's achieving or exceeding its target objective. It is as imprudent to underspend as to overspend. A sound, integrated promotion program will not be effective if arithmetically halved; nor will such a program be doubly effective if twice as much is invested. It is the professional and ethical obligation of company practitioners and agencies to develop programs that have the maximum probability of success with the most economical investment of funds. Before examining some of the ways to gauge the value of a promotion program, let us specify some of the basic principles of efficient promotion money management.

1. *Promotion budgets should be set for long-range objectives and "timed" tasks.* Company objectives and marketing objectives that are planned long-range require a concomitant planning of the promotion. A three- or four-year plan is better than a two-year plan; a two- better than a one-year plan. A "corporate" advertising program, for example, that seeks to build a company image is a virtual waste of money un-

less it can be sustained for a minimum of two or three years. Reputation, image, or familiarity cannot be built in a few months.

2. *Promotion budgets that are once set should not be abrogated.* One of the most wasteful practices is retracting, reducing, or freezing promotional budgets in the midst of a going program. If the program was soundly built, the losses and waste from stopping it or retrenching in mid-course can be disastrous.

Media advertising gains its values from repetition; it maintains the most economical exposure costs from stipulated scheduling and frequency discounts. A major share of promotion costs resides in the *preparation* of advertisements and collateral print matter. With industrial print matter, it is not uncommon for the first printed copy of a piece of literature to cost as much as the entire print run. In some trade media, ad preparation may run a quarter to a third of the entire program cost. Halting a program in an advanced stage of preparation or early operation is akin to boarding up an almost-decorated house that was built to be rented. Short-term fluctuations in business, unexpected other expense, or a decision to use promotional funds for other purposes can create the most alarming wastes in a marketing operation. Once set and budgeted, it is most economical to let a program run its course.

3. *Promotion budgets that are set should be readily available.* As will be further illustrated, a promotion program consists of a series of tools, each with an estimated price tag. The cumulative costs are the budget for the program. Since budgets are established beforehand, once the total budget for a given time period is set it should be made freely available for its intended purpose. Imposing monthly or quarterly accounting or disbursement restrictions or requiring the justification of expenditures for component parts is a debilitating and time-wasting method of promotion operation and budget control. In addition, exact cost control for each component tool of a promotion program is a practical impossibility. A program may require, for example, a stipulated media advertising program, three pieces of literature, a trade exhibit, and a moving picture. The budget is normally set before *any* copywriting or graphic production work is begun. In consequence, there is no way to forecast exactly the cost of each component. The practitioner or the agency can be held accountable for providing all the tools within a margin of plus or minus 5 to 10 percent. They cannot be held accountable for this precision on individual components.

There can be dozens of ways to evaluate the worth of a promotion program. All of them, however, will be based on the values returned to the company or the marketing program or both. Company values are as often intangible as tangible. Consequently, setting a value returned on purely corporate advertising is more difficult than justifying a budget for purely "product selling" programs. With the latter, the results are tied more directly to sales success. Certainly, a corporate program that reduces the discount the company must accept from investment bankers for the issuance of new equities has a measurable value. So, too, does a corporate image that builds stature and technological capability have a tangible value for selling highly technical and costly products. Other effects, however, such as improved industry acceptance, smoother governmental relations, and better community and personnel relations are virtually impossible to quantify in value.

In product selling programs, the promotion has a definite task: to press on the "pressure point." If it succeeds (and a well-planned, soundly implemented program will succeed more often than not)—the results are directly discernible in the field-selling results. This, however, is after the fact. Our problem for the moment is to delineate ways to put a value on the planned program at its estimated budgeted cost before it can prove itself in the field. There are a variety of ways this can be done.

In selling products, there are a number of steps and factors involved, all of which cost money.

1. Making the product's existence (or improvements) known and establishing the producer's name as the source.

2. Stimulating the call for samples, demonstrations, trials.

3. The effectiveness of first calls by the company salesmen on prospective buyers.

4. The time spent by a salesman on his first calls to acquaint the prospect fully with the product or the selling proposition or both.

5. The number of calls on different prospects that a salesman can make in a week, month, or year when travel and waiting take a great amount of his effective working time.

6. The number of different influential individuals who must be "sold" at each prospect account before the buying decision is made.

7. The number of call-backs required on a prospective account before an order is placed or a contract is signed.

8. The time spent by field salesmen in locating, identifying, and making contact with the key buying influentials at each prospective account.

9. The number of calls per week or year a salesman must make to maintain existing accounts.

10. The amount of time a salesman must invest per account to obtain a given share of the buyer's business.

11. The amount of "education," technical service, or persuasion pressure that is attendant on closing a sale.

With programs directed at Phase 1 and Phase 2 marketing problems, it is at once apparent that the promotion program can save a portion of the costs of various combinations of the above. With a Phase 3 program—expanding a customer market—where the field work is primarily the merchandising of the program, the potential effect on factors 9 and 10 is quantifiable and readily apparent.

We can then particularize a series of approaches for prejudging the value of a promotion program. They are all based on making field selling more efficient and more effective. It has been repeated often enough in industry that "advertising" (let us broaden this to "promotion") cannot make a sale. And this the practitioners readily admit. However, promotion can make direct personal selling more effective. Consequently, by measuring this increased effectiveness, steps saved, time used more profitably, we can quantify the program's worth as a budget investment. The following are the most obvious ways:

VALUE OF SALES CALLS NEEDED TO "COVER" A MARKET

In industry, most markets, geographically, are either regional or national. From the anatomy of the market, the number of accounts that make up the market can easily be determined. The number of salesmen is also known and therefore—depending on kind of product, type of market, and working methods—the number of calls available per year is a matter of simple arithmetic. On the assumption that direct calls will be the only selling force of marketing, a first look at the analysis will immediately show the adequacy or inadequacy of available manpower to cover the market—that is, to make a cold call on all the prospects that make up the market. The number of calls possible by a given sales force varies with the industry. So, too, does the cost per call. In the geographically dispersed chemicals industry, two to four calls per day have been estimated as average. Even highly efficient field men who do their own scheduling and do a lot of traveling on their own time are not able to spend on the average more than 40 to 50 percent of their work time in actual, face-to-face selling. A rough figure of $100 to $120 per day can be taken as the total cost for maintaining a man on the road.

Assuming that the marketing problem is a Phase 1 or Phase 2 type, it is relatively simple to ascertain whether the field force can cover the market at all in a reasonable period of time and if it can, at what cost. This can be compared with the cost of a promotion program involving media advertising, direct mail, and trade show exhibits that can mechanically cover the entire market and warm up the prospects as an adjunct to direct selling.

Improving the Efficiency of Finding Prospects and Identifying Influentials

In certain product-marketing situations, one problem is that not all the potential markets for a product are known. In other situations, while the prospective accounts are known, the most potent influentials in the chain of command are not. In determining markets, a field force may resort to "counting smokestacks." In searching for the interested individuals within a given company, a field man may waste two or more calls. Again, viewed in terms of the marketing objective, the value of a promotion program to identify peripheral markets or to locate the interested individuals within such accounts can be compared to the cost of doing it by means of cold calls by the field force. Inquiries from media advertising and direct mail can be screened, and the percentage of cold to "warm" calls drastically reduced.

Value in Helping to Retain Accounts

In most industrial companies, the purchasing policy for regular supply products is to maintain at least two suppliers, particularly for essential raw materials. Once an account is established, every marketing manager knows that an effort must be made to maintain it. "Out of sight, out of mind" is as true in competitive selling as it is in competitive courting. In most companies, the value of the account is carefully weighed and the amount of personal contact required to maintain it is programmed.

The cost of call-backs for maintaining an account or for improving one's share of business is a quantifiable cost. A promotion program can help reduce this cost: Reasonably frequent media advertising can "assure" a user that he has made a sound buying decision, and adroit direct mail can substantially reduce the number of personal calls required for purely maintenance selling. Again, the amount of reduction and the cost per call can be a measure of the value of the supplementing promotion.

Value of a Preferred Supplier Position

In many marketing problems involving raw materials or continuing supplies, a producer finds himself with less than equitable share of the market's business. This is a Phase 2 problem, where additional business can be obtained only by improving one's position with respect to the competition. In most instances, this situation occurs when the direct selling effort has expended its force and can do no more than maintain the subordinate position. If this is the case and the pressure point has been specified, a variety of promotion programs can be created to change the status quo. The size of the budget will depend on the value of the probable effects. For example: "What is the value of increasing our share from 12 to 20 percent of the market?" The investment is particularly warranted if it is the only resource that has not as yet been tried.

VALUE OF REDUCING THE NUMBER OF CALL-BACKS REQUIRED TO CLOSE A SALE

Sales analysis can often establish a norm for the number of call-backs needed to secure an order or contract. This varies from company to company, with the type of product, and with the quality of the field selling force. However, the number of call-backs also depends on the number of different individuals who enter the buying decision. Every industrial sales manager is acutely aware of the necessity for account penetration and the dangers of not covering those individuals who have a voice. The peripheral individuals may be far removed from the purchasing agent. They may be in management, production, or even research. A promotion program in which media advertising is one of the tools can be depended on to "penetrate" the account. By this means, product benefits and selling propositions can permeate to all levels of management. If the normal number of call-backs to close a sale has historically been seven or eight and promotion can reduce it to five or six, this will be another measure of the value of the program's budget investment.

VALUE OF REDUCING TIME SPENT PER CALL PER INDIVIDUAL

In direct selling, a sizable portion of the field man's time must be spent acquainting the various influentials with the product benefit or the selling proposition—unless through promotion he has been preinformed. Considering that there may be as many as six to ten individuals per account, preselling through a promotion program can have a significant effect on the profitable use of a field salesman's time. Instead of "informing," the field man can handle the more pertinent questions of the individual that relate to his decision to buy. The time spent per call can be devoted to prices, delivery, specification, service or matters other than "education." A reduction of a quarter of an hour of time for six individuals per account times the number of salesmen times the number of accounts and multiplied by the salesman's value per hour can return a sizable value when invested in "preselling" advertising or promotion.

VALUE OF INCREASING THE SALESMEN'S EFFECTIVENESS

As all companies know, not all salesmen are equal. Individuals in all callings have their own strengths and weaknesses. One criterion for judging a salesman's effectiveness can be the ratio of sales to the number of calls made and the amount of sales in relation to the number of accounts sold. A promotion program fitted out with effective selling tools can do much to help equalize sales performance and to maximize individual sales. A sound-slide desk presentation, a moving picture, or an effective demonstration aid can be a good investment. Its value can be equated with the value of increasing the ratio of sales to calls and with increasing the size of the individual order by a reasonable figure.

One of the most significant values of corporate advertising—though a largely intangible one—is its ability to increase the stature of the field representative. Although our concern here is to show the patterns of arithmetic that can justify product-selling promotion, it should be mentioned that corporate advertising returns measurable values. A company whose field men encounter frequent rebuffs, or who have less stature than the position of the company in its field would seem to command, or who have difficulty in penetrating an account will do well to consider a back-up corporate advertising program.

VALUE OF EXPANDING DIRECT MARKETS OR CUSTOMERS' END MARKETS

This is one of the most self-evident and easiest ways to set the value of and to justify a given promotional expense. Let us say you are a supplier of nylon bearings to makers of electrical motors, and though only 5 percent of the motors now produced have nylon bearings, the technological trend is moving slowly in that direction. It is quite easy to project the value returned by a promotion program that would accelerate the trend so that in two years instead of in five 75 percent of all motors produced would be fitted with nylon bearings.

In the same vein, say you are selling aluminum foil to a series of package producers who fabricate it into packets for salad seasonings, dehydrated soups, pipe tobacco, and pancake mix; and that you enjoy 55 percent of their business and this is the ceiling. It is not difficult to put a value on a promotion program whose objective is to convert spice producers to foil packages, or to induce soluble tea and coffee makers into offering a premeasured portion pack, or to establish foil packs of cigars, gaskets, or transistors. The value of expanding direct or customer markets is easy to assess.

In budgeting for a task, it is obvious that the initial estimated investment should take into account certain facts of life, such as how long it will take a given number of field men to call on a given number of accounts, how many inquiry follow-ups can be made by available field men, and how long it will take for media advertising to reach the publication's audience with a full, multiple-advertisement campaign. Even a high-readership advertisement will register on no more than about 30 percent of the audience with a single insertion. For the particular message, three or four repeats are prudent—and this applies for each of the messages in a campaign for a total registration.

In a long-range task program planned for three to five years, it is advisable to invest the media advertising budget most heavily in the first third of the time span.

The basic principles of establishing promotion budgets can be summed up in this sequence: Develop the program best suited to have the most significant power to press on the pressure point, design the program plan without bias in favor of particular tools, devise the program that provides the most logical tools for the total communications problem, estimate costs and see what the total price tag is likely to be. Compare this with the value to be derived from achieving the marketing objective. If the latter is great enough, the contribution that promotion can make will justify its cost.

In industrial marketing, there need be no preconceived notions of what percentage of sales should be invested in promotion, what "the company ought to do in advertising," or how it should imitate the competition. The cost of programs has no fixed relationship to their effectiveness; a soundly conceived, viable program can often be very low in cost. This does not imply that all marketing programs can be aided in their solution with minuscule cost programs. The pressure point determines the needs; the needs determine the costs. The prudence of the investment must be judged in the light of attaining the marketing objective. It is the nature of the task and the value to be derived from carrying it out that should be the sole measure of the promotion investment.

8

LAUNCHING, MAINTAINING, AND EVALUATING PROGRAMS

To this point, we have set down the fundamentals: IA&SP is the art of getting people to think and act in a predetermined way through persuasive communication utilizing the seven categories of tools. We have postulated that the discipline calls for professional competence in the craft of writing (or good critical judgment) astute employment of the graphic arts, and an esthetic sensitivity. We have established that each communication tool should first be selected, then produced with the controlling purpose: "What is this tool supposed to do?" Programs are suitable combinations of these tools deployed mechanically (in publications, through the mail, or in exhibits) and used personally by the sales representatives. Most pertinent, we have indicated that programs are productive in direct proportion to their focus on a pressure point determined from knowledge of the market, their integration in a marketing plan that assigns the IA&SP function a specified part of the selling task. The next logical step is to examine a practical method of putting the discipline to work.

One of the most prevalent weaknesses in industrial companies' use of promotion, aside from nonexistent or shaky foundations, is the divorcement or exclusion of it from an integrated sales plan. We can facetiously term this the "float" syndrome. It is most likely to exist in companies that depend on a number of outside agencies, or on one agency that has little or no interest or no profit in a complex account, or where the in-house promotion manpower is spread too thin, or where sales management pays only lip service to marketing planning. The "float" syndrome shows itself in a series of sporadic, ad hoc projects: a media advertising program that runs for a time and is abandoned or a proliferation of literature whose purposes overlap. The float syndrome sires sales brochures with exhaustive technical instructions, instructional brochures that seem bent on selling, general brochures that talk to a dozen markets. It is also characterized by chameleon-like changes of copy style, by alternately serious and frivolous approaches in graphics, and by on-again, off-again projects. It generally reflects either a lack of long-range marketing planning or an ignorance of the value of promotion in the marketing mix. Or it may simply mean the IA&SP practitioner is inept.

· To emphasize once again: The most productive use of IA&SP logically demands an integrated program, with a specific objective, focused on a definite pressure point, operated on a timed plan.

There is no stigma involved in discontinuing all promotional support for a product—aside from routine printed matter. Many companies do this, and the marketing position may warrant it. But discontinuance is only prudent at the end-point of a previously planned timed program, when none of the predetermined investment will be wasted. There *is* waste, however, in cutting off a program during its prime. Yet there is an even greater waste in the "float" syndrome—producing literature for transient needs or sudden unforeseen communication emergencies, or advertising when the mood strikes, when trouble looms, when competition surges ahead, or when some budget is available. There is also waste in creating sales tools far too elaborate for a particular undertaking.

Some promotion practitioners "live" within the marketing department; others have tenuous contact; still others dwell apart. Whatever the day-to-day interface, lucky indeed is the promotion practitioner (and the company) if the management's operating practice requires *written* marketing plans to which the promotion practitioner has access and to which he is expected to contribute. Nothing reveals so clearly the quality and quantity of market knowledge, the feasibility of a specific marketing objective, the logic of a marketing strategy as a completely written-out market anatomy, marketing plan, and sales program. Strengths and weaknesses will be apparent, and from the written information supplied, the all-important pressure point will be clearly discernible. At the same time, the sales problem is defined, the reasonableness of the marketing objective and the logic of the marketing strategy are apparent. The pressure point (the most critical element in the promotion planning) is visible, defined, and validated, and the selling tactics specified. The generalship of marketing is available for inspection, use, and performance accountability.

Launching an IA&SP Program

A practical method for promotion planning is to start with an information exchange and general discussion meeting on the subject of the marketing problem. This meeting should include the advertising agency, the in-house promotion practitioner, and the sales or marketing manager responsible for sales planning. Its purpose is to examine the marketing situation, define the sales problem, near-term and long-range, and reach an understanding on the marketing plan and its objective. In the absence of written market information, a poor second best is a description of the market and the sales problem written out by the promotion practitioner or developed in the information exchange of the meeting. If complete descriptive and quantitative market information is on file, this may be used for reference. In this fact-weighing, situation-assessing conference, the sales situation is fully explored. It should disclose the present position of the product or service in the market, the competition, the technological trends in the market, the product's strengths and weaknesses as related to customer needs, identify and quantify the customers and prospects, examine the current or planned selling proposition, and set forth the marketing goals.

This meeting concludes with the careful and meticulous writing of the pressure point.

It is impossible to overstress the importance of correctly identifying and clearly stating the pressure point. It determines how the promotion program will be conceived, built, and operated. It is the fulcrum rock for the promotion lever. It determines the program concept, the kinds of tools required, the character of the tools, the program character, size, duration, and timing. It is the most critical ingredient in formulating an IA&SP program. With a clear understanding between marketing management and the promotion practitioner of "who must be made to do what," the logic of the skeleton plan for the program, which is the next step, should be self-evident.

Armed with the information exchange of this meeting and the agreed-on pressure point, the practitioner is ready for the next step— the creative thinking out of a viable program. With an underpinning of market knowledge and a defined pressure point, most practitioners find conceiving a program to be the least arduous part of their calling. When one is faced with a load of rock that must be moved a mile, it is not difficult to see that a truck will probably be necessary. When one sees a pile of small precious stones, of which parcels of six have to be delivered to a hundred places, it does not take genius to infer that the job will probably require either messengers or insured special-delivery mail. And so with the pressure point—a problem in persuasive communication. The problem suggests its own solution—a program built with selected combinations of the seven tools of the trade.

With the pressure point as its base, a program concept is developed, in which the needed tools are specified and their cost estimated. A bare description of the program concept, tools required, and manner of operation can normally be fully written out on a single sheet of paper, and the required tools and estimated production costs appended as an itemized list. The elaborateness of the presentation of the program for marketing management approval will be a matter of company choice. Some practitioners go as far as comprehensive advertisement layouts, literature stylings, and first-draft manuscript copy. In other instances, the bare description of the tools may be sufficient.

The program concept and budget is then formally presented for approval to marketing management. Any modifications, additions, or subtractions deemed advisable, and agreed on, can be made on the spot. If this procedure is followed, rarely will the recommended program fail to sell itself. This is because every item of the program is recommended for the purpose it serves. It is because the program concept has been developed with full knowledge of the marketing problem, directed at the agreed-on objective, devised to solve the communication-persuasion problem. The program is designed for the *task*. Its budget represents a prudent businessman's risk—not much different in kind from the risk of hiring untried sales representatives. After the program has been approved by the marketing manager (and others as deemed necessary), the next step is to create the tools and field the program, fully informing the field representatives of its purpose, its mechanics, and its required follow-up.

It is advisable to hold such formal promotion planning meetings not less than once a year, progress reviews as needed. Besides providing the starting point for a new program, the periodic meetings make possible the evaluation of continuing programs.

The tools created should not be "pat" or trite. The best creative capability can and must be brought to bear in producing them. After all, the estimated budget allocation is the only restriction. Simply producing something that fits the bare requirements is not enough, whether the category be the media advertising or the demonstration aid carried by the salesman or the reminder-advertising giveaway he leaves behind. It is here that the freshest creative ideas have their most satisfying outlet—as long as the principle of aptness for the product, market, and audience is not disregarded.

Innovation for innovation's sake has no place in industrial promotion. A sales brochure for design engineers on a special alloy steel should not look like a housewares catalog from a department store. A direct mail piece on a materials-handling system for metal stampings, particularly if it's to be sent to company presidents, should neither resemble a gasoline promotion nor be filled with tables of engineering conversion factors. A sales presentation created for marketing executives of prospect companies should confine itself to information of marketing interest, not drag in irrelevant manufacturing savings and the product's close adherence to specifications.

Innovation, creativity, imagination, and judgment of the highest order will insure that solidly oriented programs will attain the maximum traction through the *excellence* of the tools.

MAINTAINING IA&SP

The maintenance of an IA&SP program requires very careful observation, judgment, and evaluation. Several cardinal guidelines can be set. First of all, to judge the strengths and weaknesses of a planned schedule, carry out a total program concept, using all the tools. Make subsequent modifications only where demonstrably needed, not out of personal bias or through making a snap judgment. If early disappointments are encountered or weaknesses show up, modify and change, but don't throw out the baby with the bath water. If a major benefit sought from the program is inquiry returns from media advertising, it may happen that inquiries are too few or that there are too many of low grade. This is not an indictment of the media-advertising tool. Instead, it may mean a weakness of publication selection, an inadequacy in the benefits promised in the advertisement, or a misunderstanding on the part of respondents of the nature of the offer. The best media analysis and schedule selection that can be done *before* a campaign begins may require modification after the advertising starts to appear. Too few inquiries (if inquiries are sought) may be the fault of an advertisement's creative approach. A flood of low-grade inquiries may be the result of ill-advised couponing, ill-advised media selection, or the wording of the spur-to-action offer (frequently much too general—as a reading of any trade magazine will reveal). Inquiries of dubious value can be mechanically screened with printed reply cards requesting more particulars about the respondents' interests, a highly advisable procedure for optimizing the value of the inquiry contacts that the field force follows up.

Additional tools may be introduced as required. One method of equalizing annual promotion expenditures for a particular program is to develop the tools from a basic sufficiency to a full variety over a reasonable time. Thus an easel flip-over presentation suitable for groups of 12 can evolve in the second year to a sound slide or a moving picture; a simple "before" and "after" sample used by field men can be upgraded to a full demonstration sample case.

In employing media advertising for constant-contact purposes in selling programs (or for building the corporate image), it is a truism that the company will often grow tired of a repeated advertisement before the audience becomes conscious of the message. If the campaign is a three-advertisement series to cover a trio of messages that give the complete story of the product benefits, and if four appearances of each advertisement are planned, the personal experience of the writer is that an appearance pattern for the three of 1, 1; 2, 2; 3, 3; 1, 2, 3 is most advisable. Since pretesting is costly, difficult for technical industrial audiences, and hardly justified by the media cost, there is no way to determine beforehand what aspect of the product benefits will register most solidly or bring the greatest response. This pattern not only makes possible additional repetitions of the strongest advertisement in a continuing schedule but can serve as a guide to the preparation of succeeding advertisements.

Two strange and bemusing sins are often committed in industrial promotion with programs that prove successful. One is to continue a program after it has run its logical course simply because it was successful. The other is to take the concept of a program that has been successful in one area and attempt to apply it in a program involving a different product or market without regard to basic differences in the sales situation or the market anatomy. This can occur in situations involving separate divisions in the same company as well as in competitive situations. All of the promotion planning concepts treated thus far indicate the probable futility and waste of such unthinking courses of action.

EVALUATING AN IA&SP PROGRAM

Evaluating a program cannot be done either in the abstract or by using esoteric standards of measurement. Evaluation is the assessment of measurable effects with respect to the program's objective. Evaluation should relate to the program as a whole, although examination of individual tools is prudent. In product-selling programs, results are more easily measurable than they are in purely corporate or image-building campaigns.

For media-advertising campaigns whose purpose is image building, a basic measure of effectiveness can be most readily quantified by comparing initial, or "benchmark," recognition and attitude studies with subsequent studies based on comparable samples of the audience. Such studies can be made by random samplings of the target industry or by using arithmetical samplings from publications' circulation lists. Qualified market and advertising researchers can advise on the sampling method and on the data-gathering method. The establishing of the sample, the type of information gathered, the method of aggregating it, and the interpretation of the results are tasks for specialists. For the IA&SP practitioner, the most critical point to observe is that benchmark and follow-up studies must be carried out in an absolutely identical manner if the results are to be compared.

With product-selling programs, the assessment can be more direct, but rarely can the results of post-program evaluation be entirely clear-cut. Even when a marketing objective has been achieved or exceeded, it is a mistake for the IA&SP practitioner to credit an excessive portion of marketing success to the promotion program. There are too many unmeasurable market factors that enter the picture. The program is part of the marketing mix. It is expected to carry out a specific portion of the sales work, and therefore evaluation should be confined to measuring that particular portion of the task that was assigned.

Pragmatically, the judgment of the field representatives is one of the most direct and dependable measures of what promotion contributes. In their daily work with their varied field contacts and the results they note from the program's component tools, the field representatives have the most pertinent evidence of how well the program works as a whole and how well its individual tools work. Closely allied will be the judgment of the sales manager responsible for the marketing operation. These evaluations far transcend any other measurement.

Yet there are a variety of other evaluation measurements. Whatever approach is employed, however, it should always be directed at performance in relation to the specific objective of the program, the "what" of the pressure point. The same applies to evaluation related to individual tools—performance must be measured against purpose.

In sound marketing practice, the marketing team's objective has been carefully planned. This might variously be increased number of new orders per quarter, more former customers recovered, larger initial orders, reduction in the number of calls required to secure a first order, a higher percentage of orders written per 100 sales calls, business taken away from competitors, reduction in average time spent per sales call, an increase in the average off-take per customer, and many others. The contributory effects of the promotion program can then be judged on the basis of what the marketing team has accomplished. For continuous supply products or services, the dollar volume, pounds, or units moved in a time period before the program starts compared to the amount for a like period after it has started is one type of measure. Another might be assessment of the market share at the start of a program and periodically as it proceeds. Yet a third might be to calculate an index of the number of calls per units sold per salesman over a period of time that precedes the program as compared with the same index during and after the program's course.

For individual tools, evaluation is the same: How well does the tool accomplish its particular purpose? A media advertising program may thus be measured by its response, by stimulation of sampling, by the requests for demonstrations and prices, by volume of product literature distributed, by the prospective purchaser's degree of buying interest when contacted, by the reception accorded salesmen, and by the product awareness that company representatives encounter in the field. The same applies to the direct mail tool. Sales presentations—in any format—that fully inform and provoke the right reactions can be rated as effective; those that cause recurring questions to be raised, incomplete; those that create misunderstandings and beget no favorable reaction, failures. Trade exhibits are measurable by their traffic, by the number of subsequent inquiries, by the number and type of new contacts established. Service devices and reminder giveaways are measurable by their popularity.

A program created for an agreed-on task, focused on the "who" of the pressure point, and furnished with tools designed for a specific use will set its own evaluation parameters. If the formulation is sound, the program will be sound and the tools justified at the outset. Such a program differs radically from programs developed without the complete rapport so essential between marketing and promotion.

9

MARKETING STRATEGIES AND THE PROMOTION COMPONENTS

The following examples of marketing tasks and sales problems illustrate the foregoing promotion concepts and methodology applied to specific situations. Where real problems or programs are cited, they have been disguised so as not to reveal the confidences of valued friends and associates. The reader is hereby assured, as in novels, that any resemblance to real companies, living or dead, and actual programs, past or present, is purely coincidental. He is also assured, however, that the methodology is very real indeed and that the program concepts are eminently practical. Scores of successful case histories are made available every year by the trade associations, by publications, by advertising agencies, and by graphic arts suppliers. While some of these are complete, many are confined to isolated tools that have some special excellence.

Our purpose in this and the foregoing chapters is to emphasize the inseparable relationship in industrial promotion between market knowledge, market problem analysis, marketing planning, and the promotion program itself. If we have succeeded in setting down a workable methodology, if these examples clarify the concepts, the soundness of the approach should convince marketing executives that the promotion discipline can be of very real assistance. And this applies to virtually any selling problem that is thoroughly analyzed. Appreciating this fact might well induce more industrial companies to dig more deeply into marketing problems and to give a larger share of the marketing workload to IA&SP. The pattern of combining analysis, logic, and creativity can also lead to more, and more effective, programs generated by advertising agencies and promotion practitioners. It can be repeated here yet again that in any industrial marketing problem—aside from pricing, poor quality, or technological obsolescence—the IA&SP discipline can provide a significant measure of assistance in its solution.

In judging the viability of a program concept based on a clearly defined pressure point, a practical formula is the same as was used in devising the product's selling proposition. The practitioner simply puts himself in the prospect audience's shoes and examines his program in the light of: "What does this do for me in terms of conviction, registered information, persuasion?" Obviously, the goal is the ultimate that can be attained on all three counts with an acceptable investment.

The following examples illustrate the interrelationship of marketing and promotion in addressing a variety of industrial marketing problems and the application of the concepts covered in the preceding chapters.

CASE 1

The Manchester Paint Corporation has been established for many years as a medium-size producer of cast-steel-product dip coatings, road marking, and marine paints. The company, seeking to diversify, has just made a survey of industrial-maintenance paint consumption. As a result of this survey, it found that chemical plants had the worst problem of corrosion control and repainted more frequently and used more paint per year than any other single industry. In consequence, it determined that chemical-making plants would be its target market, started the product R&D, and made a thorough study of this specialized market. It was learned that there were 2,800 chemical plants in the U.S. and that they consumed 1.8 million gallons of maintenance paint annually. Two of the largest paint makers in the U.S. had 35 and 30 percent of the sales respectively; the remaining 35 percent was divided among five other paint companies. None of the companies supplying paints to chemical plants was concentrating on this specific market, either in its product development or its marketing. Over 90 percent of the chemical plants used two or more suppliers' paints, primarily because this made possible a greater choice of colors. There were three contract painting firms in the field, operating in the South and Southwest, which did maintenance painting. These firms serviced about 20 percent of the industry, since they handled almost all the plants in their territory, which was heavily populated with chemical plants. These contractors bought paint on bids.

A thorough study of the market showed that the chief of maintenance or plant operating superintendent was the most influential voice in the choice of materials and all matters of plant maintenance.

The ten largest chemical companies operated 80 percent of the plants. Six of these companies, representing 55 percent of all plants, had central staff engineering departments that set standards for repainting schedules, but only one specified a particular paint supplier's brand. Thus the industry concentrations consisted of three contracting firms that serviced 20 percent of the market and ten chemical companies that represented 65 percent of the market and that were largly uncommitted to a particular brand (materials choice was locally autonomous, and four-fifths of the painting was handled by plant maintenance crews). Twenty-five chemical companies accounted for the remaining 15 percent of the market.

Manchester Paint's marketing manager studied the market and set as his marketing objective to achieve within three years a 50 percent share of the maintenance paint sold to chemical plants. He could assign only three salesmen to cover the national market. For his marketing plan, he laid out two programs:

Direct selling for standardization program.

Direct selling to interested prospects program.

As a highly market-oriented individual, he discerned several needs in the anatomy of the market. First of all, he saw that chemical plants required the greatest corrosion protection. A related consideration was that labor costs were high—the paint represented less than 10 percent of the repainting costs. He also saw that a wider color choice was needed, not for beauty but for identification.

Working with R&D, he guided development of a high quality epoxy paint with outstanding bond strength to metal. This was priced at 10 percent more than the going brands because early evaluation indicated that it would protect for at least 30 to 35 percent longer.

The marketing problem was a Phase 1 problem with two pressure points.

Pressure Point 1. The staff engineering departments of the six largest chemical manufacturers must be induced to at least recommend, if not specify, Manchester paint to their local plant maintenance chiefs.

Pressure Point 2. Chiefs of maintenance or superintendents of chemical plants must be made aware of the existence and superior longevity of Manchester paint and induced to express an interest in evaluating it.

PROGRAM CONCEPT

The marketing manager and the IA&SP practitioner agreed that Manchester paint was virtually unknown in the chemical industry. Yet they also agreed that hard economics ruled out a corporate advertising program, which could have no other value to the company than back-up for the product selling. A media advertising program, however, seemed logical. This was because as many as 7,000 to 10,000 influentials might have to be reached at the 2,800 plants, and because inquiry leads were essential for the direct selling (Pressure Point 2). As a compromise, IA&SP suggested that a "box" appear in all the ads and literature, a box giving a précis of Manchester's success with marine, traffic, and dip paints, and citing, with permission, prestigious users. The trademark "Epoxicote" was obtained—on the basis that epoxy resins and their great chemical resistance would be familiar in the chemical industry and would connote a unique basic quality. The selling proposition for Manchester Epoxicote was packaged as follows.

> • A warranty offered to provide replacement paint at no cost if an Epoxicote job failed in two years or less under any normal operating conditions.
> • A claim that an Epoxicote painting would last at least 25 percent longer than other maintenance paints under identical conditions.
> • Epoxicote would be available in white, black, and seven colors, in 55-gallon, 5-gallon, and 1-gallon drums (three colors more than the competition offered).
> • A promotional platform based on the savings in terms of the lower costs of protection per year with Epoxicote, even though the paint itself cost 10 percent more than other coatings. This was made into a copy line:

EPOXICOTE CUTS YOUR ANNUAL CORROSION
CONTROL COSTS AT LEAST 25% . . . BY SAVING
ON PAINTING, NOT ON THE PAINT

The promotion would support the sales program in the following way: Media advertising and direct mail would be used to obtain inquiry leads that would optimize field selling time for isolated accounts. Other, more intense mail would be used on the six major chemical companies' staff engineering departments. Direct selling tools would be created for the three field representatives.

PROGRAM TOOLS

1. Three full-page, two-color advertisements to appear 13 times in *Chemical Week* addressed to plant management and maintenance men, positioned in the section devoted to production. Advertisements would stress labor cost savings and long protection. The spur to action to be the offer of the . . .

2. Basic sales brochure: "Epoxicote—The Corrosion Protection Paint for Chemical Plants That Cuts Yearly Costs at Least 25 Percent." This brochure would present all the use benefits and technical performance benefits in terms of savings in overall maintenance costs.

3. A series of three first-class, personal letters to the four most influential individuals in the staff engineering departments of each of the six major chemical companies. The objective of these letters would be to obtain an appointment for a face-to-face demonstration meeting— to sell the staff, to obtain a list of the names of chiefs of maintenance of each company's plants, and also to induce, if possible, the staff engineering departments to circularize to their individual plants' maintenance heads the Epoxicote literature.

4. For these meetings, each salesman to be provided with
   • A collapsible demonstration rack on which to hang steel test plates with the seven colors in a row at the top and similar plates showing effects of 1,000-hour Weatherometer tests, immersion in 10 percent sulfuric, immersion in 10 percent caustic, immersion in saturated salt solutions.
   • A supply of hand-around steel test plates for comparison— half of the samples bonded together with Epoxicote and others with a conventional paint—to demonstrate the greater film adhesion by demonstrating the greater difficulty of separating the Epoxicote film from the metal.
   • A tabletop flip-over presentation, suitable for a meeting audience of up to ten, that would cover the quality superiority benefits of Epoxicote and conclude with three different cost comparisons of typical painting programs. This would show the relative cost savings that stem from longevity of the applied coating versus the actual material costs. This presentation would also be produced in small, desk-top format for the salesman's use with an audience of one, two, or three individuals.

• The creation of a "Maintenance Painting Cost Estimator" form that would make it easy to compute and compare costs of all factors in a maintenance painting program.

PROGRAM OPERATION

1. Returns from the media advertising are answered with the sales literature, a cost estimator form, and a courteous tip-on acknowledgment card asking respondent if the Manchester representative can arrange for a call to show samples and give prices. All returns of this tip-on card and all letter inquiries received from advertising are turned over to field representatives for approaching the contact by letter, phone, or sales call.

2. The three successive first-class letters to individuals soliciting a demonstration meeting (dropping acceptances from list for the second and third mail-outs) are sent to the headquarters engineering staffs of the six major chemical companies. As headquarters meetings are arranged and held and the company's local plants' maintenance personnel are identified, letter contact is made with the local plants to request personal contacts. These letters distribute the sales literature, and the cost estimator form. The local contacts are then followed up. If the three letters do not bring an acceptance from all six targets, a fourth sales letter is sent, which offers to supply 50 gallons of Epoxicote to be used at any plant for a comparison test in return for a response and an expression of interest.

3. After 12 months, a sales presentation is made up for the three southern contract painters. This shows the next two-year projected media advertising. It offers a quantity-purchase discount to each contract painter firm in return for its adding an Epoxicote quotation to its job bids along with its conventional material estimate and allowing the buyer to choose.

CASE 2

The Corrugated Kraft Boxboard division of the Great National Paper Company offered all grades of corrugated boxboard to shipping-case fabricators across the U.S. The Corrugated Kraft product line had become "commodity," duplicated in quality and price by eight other paper manufacturers. The box-fabricating market consisted of 50 box makers whose purchase requirements were in excess of 100 carloads a year; 245 who purchased between 50 and 100 carloads a year; and 475 who purchased fewer than 50 carloads a year. In addition, 40 food packers were making their own cases at 255 locations, consuming altogether 300 carloads a year. Because of highly competitive pricing, less and less of the division's ten salesmen's time could be devoted to selling corrugated boxboard. The 245 largest boxmakers were buying at 295 dispersed locations; the 475 smaller ones at 475 locations. Through prior aggressive contact work, quality control, and price leadership Great National had secured an enviable 20 percent of the market. However, since the sales force was forced to cut the call frequency it became apparent that, although monthly volume was rising, it was not rising as fast as total consumption. The number of actively buying accounts was practically unchanged. But Great National was not holding its share of the market. From long-time familiarity with the industry, the marketing manager was aware that practically all corrugated box manufacturers had at least three suppliers and that many had four. Further, the buying was so routine that the choice of supplier and the share of business lay entirely in the hands of the purchasing agent.

The marketing problem was a Phase 2 problem: to improve one's position with respect to competition. In studying the anatomy of the market, the marketing manager calculated that in a year the 50 largest box makers consumed about 6,000 carloads, the 245 medium-size box makers about 18,000, the 475 small firms about 14,000. It was obvious that the biggest volume lay among the medium and small box makers, and that this was where the business was being lost since the sales force had tended to concentrate on the largest producers.

The pressure point. The purchasing agents of box-making companies, and most particularly the medium and small firms, must be induced to become more favorably disposed toward Great National and to believe that it deserved a larger share of their requirements.

PROGRAM CONCEPT

In studying the anatomy of the market, the marketing manager and the IA&SP practitioner noted that the food companies making their own cases constituted a negligible segment of consumption and that the practice was not symptomatic of a trend. Actually, user-made cases were more costly in the equipment required, in space needed, and in time consumed than were purchased cases. Nevertheless, it was apparent that user-made cases for food products—which was the largest customer segment for box makers—was a disturbing industry development, particularly worrisome for medium and small box makers. A program was conceived whereby Great National took the side of the box makers and "carried a lance" for the industry.

1. A media advertising program to run for 18 months in *Food Processing* and *Packaging* magazines. Six two-color, bleed-page advertisements to run three insertions each. Each advertisement was to cover one of the six major reasons why it was more advantageous to purchase from a box maker than to make cases in the plant. The ads covered plant space saved, no investment in machinery, fewer waste cuttings of raw stock, less worker cost per unit when purchased, constricted expertise, lower efficiency for a given output. The spur to action of the advertisements was the offer of a list of Great National's customers in the respondent's state.

2. A design style and dimensioning folder. This piece of literature emphasized box makers' efficiency and expertise and illustrated all the standard design styles available in corrugated shipping cases. These were laid out in line drawings so the "buyer" could write his exact dimensions directly on the style he was ordering. This folder was designed so it could be imprinted with the customer box maker's name and be used by his representatives to clarify order writing and minimize errors.

3. A presentation for Great National's salesmen to use that displayed the six advertisements in the program, the media, and the scheduling.

4. A series of 14 direct mail pieces as follows.

• A personal letter was sent to all box makers' purchasing agents, announcing that Great National would not solicit business from any of the food packers who were making their own cases, that the company's policy would be to promote use of cases supplied by box makers, and that the company would undertake an advertising program to discourage any additional food packers from making their own cases.

• A second letter was sent, attached to a preprint of the first advertisement before its appearance, requesting permission of the box makers' customer to include the firm on the statewide lists being drawn up, and offering in return a supply of 2,000 of the design and dimension folder imprinted with the customer's name.

• Five additional letters carrying preprints of each advertisement as completed; six sample copies of the two publications with a tab-on card showing the first appearance of each advertisement in the magazine. A final mailing of the six-advertisement campaign made up into a foldout and carrying cover copy addressed to shipping case users stressing the value of a reliable supplier. The final mailing offered this wrap-up literature in quantity to the box makers' customers for their own salesmen's use.

PROGRAM OPERATION

The ten field salesmen concentrated their field time on the accounts where the losses in business were apparent from account analysis. They mentioned the company's program twice at each account in the course of the next year's calls. On these two occasions they covered first the program's concept and, later, its execution using their presentation. The major responsibility for merchandising the program was left to direct mail.

CASE 3

The Nestor Corporation produces, among a wide variety of plastics, a specialty high-strength, clear plastic trademarked Duronite, whose granules when molded, extruded, or vacuum-formed make transparent products of thin walls with a very high resistance to breakage. The plastic raw material has found a number of uses over the years, none of which has created a large volume of sales. One other producer has a similar material, but Nestor Corporation has supplied 60 percent of all of this type of material used in industry. The major consumption has been in appliance parts, small automobile parts, and in industrial meter covers. Nestor Corporation's customers for the material are primarily custom molders, who make parts on contract for other manufacturers. The consumption has been static, having ceilinged out in these three kinds of uses. Marketing has subsided to the point of simply supplying material when called for.

One day the marketing manager read of the development of a disposable hypodermic syringe that was then being tested. The syringe barrel and plunger had been molded of Duronite. A small ethical-drug manufacturer had developed the application as a convenience package for his anti-allergy serums. The sales manager followed up and contacted the pharmaceutical manufacturer. He learned that the latter considered the disposable syringe to be the coming thing in hospitals and clinics, definitely a technological trend.

The Nestor marketing manager had no contact with the ethical-drug industry, none with hospitals, none with doctors. Further, he could not undertake any R&D or marketing research expense, which in such a field he recognized would be quite expensive.

The marketing problem was a Phase 3 problem: to expand an end market by accelerating a technological trend. After a necessarily superficial analysis of the market, the marketing manager saw immediately that his 21 salesmen, who handled the company's whole line of plastics, lacked both the time and the contacts to do anything practical to foster this new development. Information indicated that while ethical-drug houses did indeed compete for the favor of doctors and hospitals on a spectrum of more or less standard medicinals, most firms offered highly specialized medicinals that the doctors accepted for their therapeutic values, not for their packaging. In addition, hospitals and doctors used a large quantity of hypodermic syringes for various size injections that could not be prepackaged. Yet these syringes required the same cleaning, sterilization, and aseptic storage for reuse. Finally, it was apparent that a range of syringe capacities would be needed and that the molds for producing these sizes would be a large, unacceptable investment for any single one of the 42 sizable drug makers. In short, his selling proposition for Nestor's Duronite in disposable syringes would require two benefits: (1) the conversion to use of disposable syringes would have to be made both easy and economical for drug makers, (2) the disposable syringes would have to be made available to doctors and hospitals for all injection uses. He designated the pressure points for promotion as three:

Pressure Point 1. A hospital supply firm and a plastics molder must be induced to form a consortium with Nestor to make disposable syringes readily available to hospitals, doctors, and pharmaceutical makers.

Pressure Point 2. Ethical-drug producers must be attracted and induced to offer their drugs in premeasured doses in disposable syringes.

Pressure Point 3. Hospitals and doctors must be induced to demand disposable syringes.

PROGRAM CONCEPT

In the whole nation, there were only six large hospital supply firms. Twenty-one of the drug makers were concentrated in the eastern third of the U.S., and there were also five large competent plastics molders in this area. Marketing estimated that contact work and tooling could be completed in 90 days. An R&D man was assigned to work out design and sizes of syringes for the industry with the pharmaceutical house that had developed the concept and to gather basic data on the cost of cleaning and maintaining supplies of sterile hospital syringes. Media advertising would be used to inform doctors and hospitals of the advantages of disposable syringes and to keep them informed of the particular drug specialties that were available. After an eastern molder was established, a western firm would be set up. The initial molders would supply all hospital supply houses and all drug firms. The hospital supply firm that agreed to join the launching consortium would be recompensed its contribution to the molds through a share of the molders' profits; Nestor would be repaid its share of investment in the molds and also 50 percent of its first year's advertising cost. The business developed would be channeled to the eastern and western molders that the marketing program would set up. By being aggressive and first, Nestor felt it could establish a franchise for Duronite syringes with pharmaceutical makers, hospitals, and doctors, and thereby hold on to a major share of the developing business.

PROGRAM TOOLS

1. A flip-over sales presentation in modular form, the basic module to cover the benefits of disposable syringes to the hospitals and doctors and pharmaceutical makers. An additional module to show an estimate of the potential market size. Another two modules, one addressed to a hospital supply firm, the other to a plastics molder proposing the formation of a consortium.

2. A media program to hospital administrators in *Modern Hospital* magazine, three advertisements run four times each the first year stressing the savings, safety, and convenience of disposable syringes.

A media program in the *American Medical Journal* publicizing the advantages—time savings, exact premeasured doses of specialties, reduced danger of carryover infection—with disposable syringes, and with a boxed news listing that would itemize the proprietary specialties as they were made available in Duronite syringes. One basic advertisement to appear every issue with a progressively updated column box for listings.

3. A basic piece of sales literature suitable for doctors, hospital administrators, and pharmaceutical firms. This to stress all the benefits of disposable syringes made of Duronite, the sizes available, and listing the hospital supply firms that took on the line.

4. A direct mail program of three first-class personal letters addressed to the presidents and marketing directors of the 42 ethical pharmaceutical firms. The first letter, attached to the literature, to announce the availability of disposable Duronite syringes in the various sizes. A second letter, attached to preprints of the demand-building ad-

vertisements being run in the hopsital and medical field. A third letter, to carry the cumulative box listings of the drug specialties now being offered in premeasured, disposable Duronite syringes and a request to carry any of the recipient's products so offered. This "box" listing as it increased in size was excellent evidence of the technological trend; it informed prospect drug makers of what *their* competition was doing.

One Nestor salesman to be assigned full time to acting as liaison between pharmaceutical makers, hospital supply houses, and the molders.

CASE 4

The Electro Weld Company manufactures and supplies welding machines and welding rod. It has a variety of specialized machines for automatic and manual seam and spot welding, and sells a full line of various metal and alloyed welding rod. The company is in competition with four other producers of machines and rods and seven firms that make and sell only welding rod. Rod sales are the most profitable part of the business, and also the most competitive. The grades of rod have become standardized, as have the sizes, packing, and performance specifications. The market for machines and welding rod is spread across the entire metals-working industry. The major buyers are the 120 automobile, truck, and car body plants; the 27 farm equipment plants; the 160 process-equipment fabricators that make boilers, heat exchangers, autoclaves, storage tanks; the 35 plants that make business machines; and the 80 plants that make large home appliances. Since welding rod is virtually a commodity, the decision maker selecting the supplier in each of the customer or prospective-customer plants is the purchasing agent.

Electro Weld has five salesmen who are kept busy handling quotations and servicing calls for new machines—but who in all their field contact try to make calls and secure continuing business on the welding rod used. However, over the past two years Electro Weld rod has lost ground even in the face of increased manufacturing activity.

The marketing problem is a Phase 2 problem—to improve the company's supply position with respect to competition. The analysis of the pressure point was obvious.

Pressure point. The purchasing agents of 487 metal-fabricating plants must be convinced that they should buy greater amounts of welding rod from Electro Weld and must be given a real inducement to do so.

Program Concept

The IA&SP practitioner pointed out to the marketing manager that an effective promotion program could only be developed by creating a very tangible "extra" service related to Electro Weld rod. This would have an assessable value—on the basis that if the company could increase its market share by 5 percent, a sum of $10,000 spent for promotion would be an excellent investment. Thus the program-concept problem boiled down to what kind of service could be created that could be financed for no more than this amount. The problem was explored with Electro Weld's R&D engineers. They pointed out that while the rod is simple, the art of welding is not. There were many problems—crystallizing, possible hidden flaws, flow of metal, and so forth. They also pointed out that in developing automatic machines they had recourse to electron-microscope examination of welds, X-ray diffraction, and radioisotope tracing. In fact, the company had a large investment in weld analysis equipment and had developed a variety of techniques for analyzing welds that few fabricators could afford to carry out. There was also a special technique of dosing any grade of welding rod with tiny amounts of radioactive metal and analyzing the finished weld with geiger counters and sensitized photographic plates. It was apparent that such technology made available to customers on an equitable basis would be a very real extra service. An alternative service, the checking out of the efficiency of a customer's automatic welding operation, was discarded. The offer of the analysis technology was chosen as the extra service.

Program Tools

1. A basic brochure entitled: "Weld Analysis . . . a Special Service for Users of Electro Weld Rod." This brochure described the kinds of problems the analysis could help solve. It also showed the technique of using isotope-tagged rod and the kinds of information it revealed on the welding operation and the weld joint itself. The service was given a specific price on an hourly consulting basis. The brochure also contained—and was thereby more valuable—a compilation of metals properties, metals actions, melting points, crystallizing points, metals compatibility, metals conductivity, and other tables for fabricating designers and engineers often referred to in handbooks.

2. A credit-stamp folder with blank spaces for credit stamps whose value could be applied for using the service. Special credit stamps were printed with the Electro Weld logo and the value in hours of service.

3. A desk-top salesman's presentation that explained both the service and how purchases of the Electro Weld rod built up credits for its use.

4. A two-letter direct mail campaign to purchasing agents. A first letter, to explain the new "Weld Analysis" service, was accompanied by the brochure. One letter enthusiastically promoted the value the service offered to the fabricating company's production foremen and the engineers responsible for quality fabrication. The letter advised the purchasing agent that the technical men would be most interested in his informing them of the availability of the service. A second letter provided the purchasing agent with the credit-stamp folder with a single stamp affixed. This letter confirmed that credits for use of the service would be issued equitably upon specific quantity purchases of Electro Weld rod. These credits should be routed from his desk to the department which from time to time would want to use the consulting service.

PROGRAM OPERATION

The first letter announcing the service sent to customers and prospects was so timed as to arrive within five days before a sales call. On the sales call, the representative went through the presentation of the service. He provided a supply of the brochures describing the service for the purchasing agent's use in informing all his company engineers concerned. The salesman then explained how future purchases of Electro Weld rod could build up credits to reduce or entirely pay for the service. Within two days of the salesman's call, the second letter, with a first "complimentary" credit stamp, was mailed to the purchasing agent. This mailing and call program continued until the entire field had been covered. Analysis reports, when the service was used, were mailed to the user in care of the purchasing agent.

CASE 5

The Power Gear & Control Company manufactures a complete variety of gears of all sizes and designs and a variety of gear motors that offer a range of power reduction. The company's products found vastly differing uses in a wide range of markets—from home appliances to specialized packaging machines, from machinery in the garment industry to farm equipment, from motorcycles to marine engines, and in virtually every kind of powered product in between.

Most of the company's business came from custom-building special units for a particular customer for a special application. Over the preceding five years, the company had developed an excellent line of "stock" gear motors and speed-reduction and power step-up gear boxes. One of these was usable on the average in one out of three needs that came to the company's attention. Power Gear was well known and respected by 250 firms for which it had performed custom work in the past. Its seven salesmen, all highly qualified mechanical engineers, maintained regular contact with all the influential individuals responsible for product design and production in this group of accounts. They also solicited business from new firms. Nevertheless, the marketing manager of Power Gear noted by using several pertinent indexes that although sales were increasing yearly, they were not keeping pace with competition. He found that he had no large markets, but was supplying custom-made gear service to many markets. The ready-to-use units were in the same position. The major marketing problem was that the need for custom gears, power-reduction motors, or control units was sporadic and diffuse. The only time such products were needed—and therefore purchased—was in the initial design of a new power product or in a product's redesign. There was no way to know, predict, or measure this. Further, the turnover in industry had the effect of taking up a great deal of salesmen's time, for it was necessary to maintain rapport with both former and current customers. The marketing manager felt it imperative to enlarge the number of contacts and set the objective as an increase of at least 100 percent.

The marketing problem was a Phase 1 problem: to inform the potential users of the existence of Power Gear's custom service and standard products and to induce them to identify themselves. The marketing manager analyzed the problem and defined the pressure point.

Pressure point. Design engineers and power-machinery development men in the widespread and diversified original-equipment manufacturing companies must be made aware of Power Gear's capability for providing custom-made power-control units and reminded of the availability of the variety of standard units that would fill many of their needs.

PROGRAM CONCEPT

In discussing the pressure point, the marketing manager pointed out that he could not afford to underwrite an expensive promotion program. Since sales were sporadic, he feared that a heavy constant-contact program would be too expensive. The IA&SP practitioner pointed out that the nature of the "who" in the pressure point dictated that media advertising must be used—but that he had conceived a way to build

109

additional traction into a reasonable media program. Basically, his plan was to use the media advertising to secure as many respondents per appearance as possible regardless of their immediate need for power-control equipment and to keep Power Gear products and capability alive in their minds after contact was made. He pointed out that the company sales catalog that was periodically reissued should be supplemented by additional reference material that would be highly useful to engineers employed by original-equipment manufacturers. In conference with Power Gear's R&D engineers, the following items were developed.

PROGRAM TOOLS

1. A series of four wall charts, well designed and headed with Power Gear's name. District field men's offices and phone numbers were prominently displayed, as was the company's offer to collaborate on any power-control problem.

One chart gave data at a glance on helical gears and the relationship of diameter, pitch, and torque. The second chart treated conventional gears. The third chart treated hypoid gears. The fourth chart was made up like a nomograph and related power requirements and speeds to a center axis on which were positioned the company's standard gear motors and standard speed-reducer products that would come closest to the power input and speed requirements. These charts were suitable for mounting on a wall or for inserting under the glass of a desk. Much time and effort was devoted to make these charts into the most useful, easy-to-read reference devices available.

2. A media advertising program was developed for *Product Engineering* and *Materials Engineering* magazines. Four black-and-white advertisements were prepared. These emphasized the company's custom capability, its standard speed reducers, power converters, and gear motors. Each advertisement was couponed and offered the reader one of the reference charts. The advertisements were run three times each in both magazines over a period of twelve months.

3. A simple, attractive newsletter format was developed for use in publishing a brief, informative report on a specific power-control problem, its alternative solutions, and how it had been solved best by Power Gear equipment.

PROGRAM OPERATION

The company salesmen presented each of their established contacts with one chart on a regular call while the advertisement offering that chart was current. They pointed out the reference value and suggested that it be wall-mounted. After the call, the salesman mailed back to the company's promotion department a card with the names of individuals contacted at each account. These cards created a mailing list to which a different case-history newsletter was sent every four weeks. Respondents to the media advertising were mailed the wall chart the advertisement offered. The highly technical nature of the offer tended to self-screen the respondents. The ad response requests were turned over to the area field representative, who, by letter, telephone, or call (depending on the importance of the company and individual), followed up. With the new worthwhile contacts he made in this follow-up, the field man qualified individuals for receiving the newsletter and added them to the constant contact mailing list. He also posted them as new call points in his regular contact work.

CASE 6

The Coated Fabric Corporation manufactures a line of vinyl-coated fabrics. These are sturdy, durable, leather-like materials with an extremely pleasing texture and good pliancy. The company can produce a variety of surface finishes and a virtually limitless color range. Its major business has been to supply materials to furniture manufacturers, automobile makers, and to luggage producers. The company wants to add at least one major new market and has selected the shoe industry. There are 17 other fabric-coating firms in the field. CF was aware that the 35 large shoe-manufacturing firms, which produced over 80 percent of the country's footwear, had been regularly solicited by other vinyl-coated fabric producers. In his study of the shoe market, the marketing manager learned that shoe company designers and marketing directors were the most influential individuals in the selection of materials. He also learned that when a new material was considered, a shoe manufacturer had to know how the material sewed and glued, how long it wore, and how well it breathed to allow the passage of air. He also learned that weight, surface texture, and colors were all related to design. As he summed up the situation: "We can make anything they want, but we have got to know what they want."

The marketing problem was a Phase 1 problem: to inform the shoe-manufacturing market of the existence of the company's materials and stimulate their interest in evaluating them.

Pressure point. The designers and marketing directors of the 35 largest shoe manufacturers must be made aware of the unique materials that Coated Fabric could supply and induced to consider them for their brands where applicable.

In discussing the sales problem with his IA&SP practitioner, the marketing manager pointed out that advertising in the shoe-industry trade magazines had been tried by several of the company's competitors whose quality was inferior to CF's—with the result that the shoe industry was already well aware that vinyl-coated fabrics were available but had never seriously considered them. Further, the company could only afford a small promotion budget.

The IA&SP practitioner said that in terms of the pressure point the designers and marketing managers had to be made aware of the company and its materials and he would propose quite a different approach. Specifically, it would seem wise as a start to retain for a day or two a consultant who was an expert on the shoe industry to determine where the vinyl-coated materials best fitted into the shoe manufacturers' needs.

This was done. The consultant stated that CF materials would be best suited for low-priced shoes for leisure wear rather than dress, for babies' shoes, and casual house slippers. He explained that materials and designing went hand in hand and theorized that perhaps one reason the shoe industry had never adapted vinyl-coated fabrics was that any one type or weight of material would be suitable for no more than one kind and one style of shoe.

PROGRAM CONCEPT

The IA&SP department contacted five university art schools and offered a $500 grant to each for a series of 30 designs rendered in color to include women's casual sport shoes, teenage girls' play shoes, babies' shoes, and men's and women's house slippers. A large variety of samples, along with complete information, was furnished to each school as study material for the advanced students. Out of this design program, 150 styles of these four kinds of shoes were returned to the company, which agreed to pay $100 to the student designer if his design went into manufacture. Ultimately, one of the outstanding students was commissioned to design a unique travel slipper that could be made in only the three basic sizes of small, medium, and large, and yet fit all wearers in each size. This design showed both sewing and gluing construction to demonstrate the fabricating versatility of CF's materials.

Out of the 150 designs created, a starting presentation of 30 was prepared.

1. A 30" by 40" coated fabric sample display presentation made up to show the great range of weights, surface finishes, textures, and colors of CF materials.

2. A presentation produced in both slide form and as a flip-over that displayed the 30 selected art school designs of leisure, baby, and slipper models.

3. A large supply of the travel slippers to serve as reminder advertising giveaways and demonstration of fabricating versatility.

PROGRAM OPERATION

The marketing manager appointed a special representative for the contact work in the shoe industry. This representative first approached one of the largest shoe manufacturers, as a customer, to place an order for 1,500 pairs of the travel slippers. Placing the order necessitated contact with the shoe manufacturer's marketing department and designers, at which a presentation was made of the CF sample materials and the designs applicable for each type of shoe.

Thereafter, group meetings with marketing people and designers at each of the remaining 34 prospects were arranged. The purpose of the meetings was to present the series of unique designs CF had developed. The potential of the company's materials was explained, the designs shown, and giveaway slippers distributed. Any design that appealed to the prospect was taken out and left with him for his exclusive use. The designs taken out were replaced with others from the reserve. The program made possible a full-dress presentation of CF materials; the giveaways showed how the materials were fabricated and how they looked in a finished product; and the wide range of designs showed the esthetic possibilities of CF materials in the four types of footwear for which they were best suited.

CASE 7

The Lancaster Process Controls Company has been in business for half a century, manufacturing meters for direct reading and recording of temperatures, pressures, liquid flow rates. The company has a complete line of standard meters that will cover virtually all processing conditions. It avoids building special systems by policy, referring custom business to another meter firm which in turn recommends a standard

Lancaster meter when the conditions can be met by an off-the-shelf product. There are three other meter makers that, among them, duplicate practically all of Lancaster's line. Lancaster has 10 salesmen who constantly keep in contact with 75 chemical engineering consultants and the engineering departments of 500 major chemical, food, paint, and detergent manufacturers. Roughly half the business consists of replacement meters; the balance is in new installations. Since Lancaster has a full line of meters for practically any set of processing conditions, its representatives can average only two calls a year on all the individuals in the roughly 600 firms in its actual and potential market. Hundreds of prospects cannot be contacted. The competition has tended to specialize more in its calls and Lancaster knows new business is slipping away.

Over the years, the company has maintained a steady corporate advertising program in *Chemical Engineering* and *Chemical Processing* magazines, running advertisements that both showed the dependability of their various products and built an image of Lancaster equipment as the standard for accuracy and long service. In analyzing its marketing position, however, Lancaster's marketing director was amazed to learn that meters had become so generally standardized that the higher echelon engineers in the processing industry no longer specified a particular brand. Their design work merely specified the range of conditions to be metered; the actual choice of brand and procurement was left to junior engineers who were in training for more responsible design tasks. The marketing manager set a target of increasing the specification of Lancaster meters by at least 15 percent in two years.

The marketing problem was a Phase 2 problem: to improve the competitive position.

Pressure point. The junior engineer specification writers in the engineering departments of major processing plants must be strongly reminded of and induced to specify Lancaster meters.

PROGRAM CONCEPT

A research study of 50 representative firms showed that the average specification writer stayed on the job two years, that 75 percent were chemical engineers out of school less than one year, and that for 85 percent this was their first job after graduation. Further, depending on the size of the firm and the quantity of work, the specification writer might control from $10,000 to $50,000 worth of meter business annually. On the basis that the replacement meter business had an odds-on chance of being the same brand, the promotion program was concentrated on the specification writers for new process equipment. The objective was to lodge the image of Lancaster in the minds of the young engineers who would specify meters and to dispose them favorably toward the company.

Because there were approximately 750 specification writers now on the job and several thousand more in their senior year at college or in graduate study, the IA&SP practitioner recommended a $25,000 reminder-advertising program.

PROGRAM TOOLS

1. The company's R&D staff and a leading professor of engineering developed a series of 20 process-control problems involving temperature, flow rate, and inline pressures. These problems were illustrated with blank-faced meters set in a schematic flow diagram. Each blank meter had "Lancaster" printed on its face or rim. The solution of the problem was recorded by drawing in what the meter reading would be under the conditions stated by the problem. These problems and the formats were devised to be unique teaching aids; they were attractively printed and tastefully identified with Lancaster.

2. Two direct mail letters were sent to the chemical engineering departments of all engineering schools.

3. A special "slide rule" was created that related ranges of pressure, temperature, and flow rate measurements to the specific Lancaster meter that would report that range.

4. A competent sculptor was commissioned to model three small figures symbolizing pressure control, temperature control, and "flowing liquid" on a base on which were mounted a thermometer, a hygrometer, and a barometer. The Lancaster company name was worked into the design of the base. This was then molded in ivory plastic to make an unusual and highly attractive desk or office ornament.

PROGRAM OPERATION

Twice a year, a two-letter mailing offering the teaching aids was sent to the universities, the second letter carrying samples of the problem materials. Quantities sufficient for classroom use were sent on request, along with an acetate overlay "key" that enabled the teacher to check the correctness of the solutions rapidly and easily.

The Lancaster salesman made a point of calling on the specification writers at each firm, supplying each with the Lancaster slide-rule meter selector. At the same time, he carried samples of five of the "problems" and advised his contacts that if they solved any three of the five correctly they were entitled to the Lancaster desk ornament. This was tactfully followed up until over the following two years most of the on-the-job specification writers had received this attractive reminder of Lancaster meters. The offer was also extended to new men as they came on the job.

CASE 8

The Loft Packaging Products Company had built its business on supplying a variety of machines for packaging cookies and compartmented box candy. These machines were designed to take "blank," flat, and die-cut boxes and assemble, fill, and wrap them. The company determined that it must diversify by going into other kinds of packaging and that it would develop basic machines that could start with raw materials rather than semifabricated material.

The R&D program was developing a machine that, starting with foil rolls, would make various sizes of envelope packs; another that, starting with rolled plastic sheet, would vacuum-form, fill, and cap various shapes and sizes of plastic containers; another that, starting with wax-coated paperboard, would cut, assemble, fill, and label-wrap frozen foods. Loft Packaging was well respected in the candy-manufacturing and commercial-baking industries. Beyond this, however, it was virtually unknown. The company management had in mind expansion of the machinery line as well as several acquisitions, primarily printing facilities and box and shipping-case manufacturing operations. The company's common stock was traded on the American exchange and there was no company debt outstanding. For the ambitious expansion program, however, management knew it would have to attract fresh capital.

The Loft marketing manager, the R&D manager, and the company president held a review meeting, after which it was announced that the machine that would make vacuum-formed plastic containers was ready to be introduced to its markets. The basic R&D work had been done through working with packagers of individual servings of jelly. As it now developed, however, the machine would handle volumes up to pint size of any semiliquid and would make cylindrical or rectangular containers within a wide range of dimension limits. The minimum cost for the machine was $75,000. R&D reported that the machine would find a vast number of packaging applications—in such dairy products as ice cream, specialty sundae confections, yogurt, sour cream, and cottage cheese; in margarine and cooking fat packaging; in cheese products and flavored dip packaging; in frozen chicken livers and frozen shrimp; and in such specialty convenience foods as individual servings of fruit jello, mayonnaise, jelly, catsup, mustard, and consommé. However, no in-depth study of any of these potential markets had as yet been made. R&D had thoroughly surveyed the mechanical art and was certain that the new Loft Former & Filler was faster and more versatile, that it was a complete new system, and that it required less operating attention than any other machine on the market. However, it was almost twice as costly as other machines that were simply fillers and cappers.

In discussing the problem of introducing it, the marketing manager set forth the most pertinent facts. A thorough study to determine the potential demand for the machine in all of its various markets would take a minimum of six months and cost an estimated $20,000 to $30,000. Thereafter, it would be essential to have machines installed and in operation so that they could be inspected by interested prospects. The machines would represent a capital investment, hence would require a buying decision by a prospect's top management. In addition, the initial purchase of the machine would require technical service if it were to be fitted in with the buyer's process and adapted to his particular packaging design—an operation that would mean effort and risk for the prospect. Inasmuch as Loft was unknown in the industries for which the machine was intended there would be some reservation about buying capital equipment from an unknown unless performance could first be amply demonstrated. The marketing manager estimated that once he had ten machines in regular operation, subsequent selling would be much easier. And, further, when he had some indication of the degree of interest in the various markets, he would be able to start thorough market analyses on the most promising for information as a base for long-range marketing plans.

The R&D manager stated that the next new machine would be ready within 18 to 24 months. The president pointed out that it would be highly advisable to get the new Former-Filler on the market as fast as possible to generate more sales dollars. Within 18 months, he estimated that the company would have to raise more capital, and added that it hoped to do so most prudently by the issuance of convertible preferred stock.

The marketing problem was a Phase 1 problem: to communicate the existence and benefits of a new product and induce interested prospects to identify themselves.

As top management and marketing management analyzed the interlocked company and marketing problem, two pressure points were designated:

Pressure point 1. Top management men in the cheese, dairy, poultry, seafood, cooking fat, and portioned-food distributing industries must be made aware of the existence of the Loft Former-Filler and at least ten must take immediate action to have one installed.

Pressure point 2. The investment bankers must be made aware of the new machinery developments at Loft that promised increased sales and faster growth and must be persuaded to underwrite capital-raising requirements on the most favorable terms possible.

The Loft IA&SP manager and the company's agency studied the two pressure points. They proposed that promotion could readily accomplish the first task within 60 days if marketing would develop a dramatic selling proposition for the first 10 installations. After discussion, marketing agreed that Loft would ship and install the first 10 machines for 60 days' operation at no cost to the prospect manufacturer and after the demonstration period would offer a lease or buy proposal.

PROGRAM CONCEPT

Neither the image required for backing up the selling of capital equipment nor the image sought in the financial community could be created quickly. However, a fast response start-off was necessary in order to get ten machines in operation. The cost of this seeding advertising should not be lost to the longer-term corporate program.

The attractive selling proposition provided a variety of "hooks" that would provide valuable material for the image-building task. It also offered a dramatic means for the corporate program to define specific markets and generate valuable leads for interested prospects.

PROGRAM TOOLS

1. A media advertising program initially scheduled for 18 months that would run in *Fortune, Time* (eastern U.S. regional editions) and *Business Week* magazines. Four advertisements would be created: one announcement, 1-page, 2-color; one 2-page spread, 2-color; two testimonials, 1-page, 2-color.

Advertisement No. 1

Headline and Subhead

THESE LOFT MACHINES HAVE SAVED BAKERS
AND CONFECTIONERS MILLIONS
OVER THE LAST QUARTER CENTURY

NOW, LOFT ANNOUNCES A COMPLETELY NEW CONCEPT
FOR PACKAGING SEMILIQUID PRODUCTS

This advertisement was illustrated with standard Loft machines with small descriptive cutlines.

The body copy of the advertisement described the general use benefits of the new Former-Filler—but did not illustrate the machine. The advertisement's "spur to action" was written: "For complete details watch for our advertisement in the [date] issue of this magazine."

Advertisement No. 2

The two-page spread used advertisement No. 1 with the action slug routed off for its left-hand page and added a right-hand page, headlined:

THE FORMER-FILLER
makes, fills, closes, seals your package
in a continuous automatic operation.

This advertisement was illustrated with a picture of the new machine, cutlined with its features. The body copy described the kinds of packages it would make and the types of products it would handle. The advertisement offered to send descriptive literature.

A separate boxed message carried this offer: "If you package over 5,000 units per day of any of these kinds of products, your firm can be awarded 60 days of absolutely no-cost packaging to demonstrate the Former-Filler. Write us immediately of your interest. Loft Packaging Products Company will select from the first week's letters responding to this advertisement five companies to receive a Former-Filler. Machines will be shipped, geared to your product and package design and operated entirely at our expense for 60 days. To qualify, letters of request must be signed by an officer of your company. Clip this printed offer to include with your letter."

The subsequent two single-page ads were devoted to two "successful" case histories of the new machine ultimately obtained from the free trials. A modified single-page Former-Filler advertisement and the two case-history advertisements were repeated three times each during the next sixteen months.

2. A basic sales brochure on the Former-Filler. The last page and inside back cover of this brochure carried a concise display and historical vignettes of earlier Loft machines.

3. Three direct-mail sales letters: the first, a general mailing that was personalized; the second, a contact-warming sales letter for answering high-quality inquiries; the third, an ad hoc sales letter for the selected "trial firms."

4. An exhibit stand planned for the forthcoming year's packaging show with a continuous five-minute film showing the machine in operation and samples of a wide variety of the packages it could produce.

The two-page spread with the "free packaging service offer" was pre-printed at the same time as the one-page "teaser" advertisement. The "teaser" was scheduled to appear simultaneously in all three publications. This appearance would generate a fair amount of inquiries. To the best of these inquiries were sent a sales letter, a slick paper preprint of the "free offer" advertisement, and the product literature. To less promising inquiries were sent a sales letter and the product literature. A file of the first promising inquiries that had been sent the preprint was set up. From the return letters from prospects who acted on the free offer *before* it appeared in the publications, five "trial" firms were selected. Their response to the mailed teaser had indicated very high interest. After the "free offer" advertisement appeared, the Loft marketing director selected the five most promising from the first week's returns. All respondents to the publication advertising who were not accorded the free trial were sent cordial personal letters and the sales literature, and an appointment for sales contact was requested.

The ten trial companies thus obtained were spread across the dairy, cheese, poultry, and prepackaged individual food-serving industries. This gave Loft technical service men experience with the spectrum of materials. In awarding each trial, it was made conditional that Loft could bring five visitors (from noncompetitive firms) to see the Former-Filler in operation—during the trial or for a period of up to one year afterward. Loft would also be allowed to take pictures and advertise the performance of the machine in the application. The entire inquiry return from the first two advertisements was analyzed to determine the degree of interest in the various areas of use as a guide to individual market study.

CASE 9

The Apex Fastener Company supplies a complete line of staples, metal screws, wire and strip-metal case strapping, nuts and bolts, and a variety of patented specialty fasteners. Its customers are in the automotive, household appliance, business machine, and toy industries. The company has been in business for 50 years and has secured a good position in each of its markets. The majority of its fasteners have stiff competition from virtually identical products, yet for a few of its patented specialties there is no competition, and companies that use them have adapted them to their product methods. However, the sale of these specialties is not profitable unless the account takes a substantial portion of the undifferentiated fasteners as well. Salesmen called regularly to maintain business and worked on new accounts.

Apex's marketing manager ran into a knotty problem. A salesman recently transferred into one of the high-volume territories was beset by acute personal problems. This caused him to slough off service requests, miss appointments, forget price quotations, and fail to meet shipping deadlines. Moreover, his irritable manner deeply offended the purchasing agents. This was discovered only after a number of orders were canceled and one offended buyer wrote in to headquarters to say that the Apex man was to call on him no longer. Though the Apex marketing manager immediately assigned a new man to the territory, there were 85 accounts, and it was hard at this point to assess the degree of damage.

The temporary marketing problem was a Phase 2 problem—to improve the company position with respect to competition. However, the specific task was to soothe all the people who might have been offended and rebuild goodwill. A minimum of $85,000 and a possible $500,000 of annual fastener business was at stake. The marketing manager reasoned that $10,000 would be a good investment if Apex could recoup position by some promotional means.

Pressure point. The purchasing agents of 85 accounts must be induced to think well of Apex, to feel cordial to the new salesman, and if offended by his predecessor, be made to forgive and forget.

PROGRAM CONCEPT

The IA&SP practitioner pointed out that although business gifts were normally frowned on and were touchy business, nevertheless if handled in a light vein and in good taste—that is, if they provoked a smile and appeared to be an advertising or promotional device—were generally acceptable. On the basis that approximately $100 could be spent on each individual, he suggested a direct mail program in which four reminder-advertising gifts would be sent out over the following five months.

PROGRAM TOOLS AND OPERATION

1. An updated version of the company's catalog and price list.
2. Direct mail send-outs as follows:
    (a) A jumbo-size postcard announcing the appointment of the new salesman. The postcard copy made the most of: APEX ANNOUNCES A NEW "SPEED-COURTESY" CUSTOMER SERVICE. The card asked the recipient to tear off the postcard's tab, drop it in the mail, and to note how fast the new catalog and price

list would reach him. The new catalog was inserted into a handsome leather correspondence carrier that was a "takeout" compartment of a matching attaché case. The correspondence carrier had the recipient's name stamped on the flap. The postcard and the letter carrier were mailed out eight hours apart so that each recipient would receive the new literature at the same time, within hours, or at the latest, the next day—whether he had sent in the request or not.

(b) Within a week, a second jumbo postcard was sent out. The copy, in a humorous vein, reported that the SPEED-COURTESY service was now operating more smoothly. The second message stated that part of the information that was to have gone out with the catalog and price list had been left behind because of too much speed. However, the new salesman would deliver it on his next call. The attaché case, with the recipient's name stamped in the leather, was packed with an attractive display card on which were mounted the Apex specialty fasteners and a selection of the most generally used fasteners. The field man gave this to each purchasing agent and assured him that the company was making a concentrated effort to improve its contact and supply service.

(c) Within five weeks, each individual on the list was sent a special cake with a card enclosed in celebration of the Apex company-founding date. It gave assurance of constantly improving service in appreciation for business.

(d) Six weeks later, a young apple tree (20″ high) was mailed to everyone on the list with a current price list of Apex fasteners. It was accompanied by a card expressing appreciation for past business and expressing the hope that future business would increase in proportion to the amount the tree grew each year— when planted according to the enclosed directions.

CASE 10

The Central Glass Matt Corporation produces fibrous glass mat which is used to make reinforced plastic products. A major use of the glass mat is the manufacture of translucent corrugated building panels. Central Glass supplies material to 65 small- to medium-size manufacturers of building panels. Except for color, the panels made throughout the industry are standard sizes with lengths, widths, and corrugations designed to match galvanized steel and aluminum panels. Central Glass is the largest of three fibrous glass producers and has 60 percent of the panel maker's business. The panel manufacturing market is one of the company's largest single markets. The 65 customer manufacturers that constitute it sell their reinforced plastic panels directly to users, to distributors, and to building supply dealers. The ultimate customer is the professional architect specifier, the builder, the contractor, and the do-it-yourself homeowner.

In a study of the market, Central Glass's marketing manager concluded that growth was being slowed by several factors: Architects were not getting sufficient technical information on the physical properties, construction characteristics, and strength properties of the panels; contractors and carpenters required instruction on how to join, mount, and fasten; and the homeowner had no design guidance for using the panels.

The marketing problem was a Phase 3 problem—to increase the size of the end-market that used the raw material. As the marketing manager analyzed the need, he defined this as the—

Pressure point. The sales departments of our 65 customers must be assisted to inform and educate building professionals on the technicalities of reinforced plastic panels and to promote more aggressively their utilitarian and esthetic values.

PROGRAM CONCEPT

In reviewing the market's anatomy and the pressure point, the IA&SP practitioner pointed out that a variety of sales tools were needed whose creation was beyond the practical capability of any one of the direct customers. In consequence, if Central Glass would create an effective series of sales tools for the industry, these could be provided on an equitable shared-cost basis to all the company's customers. However, these tools would have to be so designed as to be acceptable to the majority of customers. This meant the printed matter would have to avoid specific color representations and relate technical information to ranges of values that were pegged to selected thicknesses and glass mat content. With this as a base, Central Glass could capitalize a full program, accept a portion of the cost, and spread the remainder among all the participating customers.

PROGRAM TOOLS

1. A 20-minute voice-over motion picture that dramatically showed the characteristics of the panels, gave a short sequence on the sawing, drilling, and installing methods, and then took the viewer on a tour of 50 useful and attractive installations that represented the range of beneficial uses.

2. An architect's reinforced plastic panel reference folder that gave full technical data on the three most generally produced thicknesses and two levels of glass content.

3. A "Carpenter's Guide for Installing Reinforced Plastic Panels," a folder that clearly explained and illustrated the methods of construction.

4. A series of building plans illustrating well-designed, attractive structures with dimensioned construction plans:

- Four different plans for a garage.
- Four different styling plans of swimming-pool privacy screens.
- Four plans for covered patios.
- Four plans for carport enclosures.
- Four plans for milking sheds and barns.

5. Three sizes of newspaper advertisements in mat form promoting plastic panels and offering the plans for sale at a small cost. Advertising mats were laid out in such a way that dealers' names could be inserted.

All printed matter was designed so that quantities could be supplied individually imprinted with the panel customer's name and his trade signature for his panels.

PROGRAM OPERATION

Central Glass Matt funded the production of all promotion materials. A print of the moving picture was given to each customer for his use and regional circulation. A kit showing the entire series of printed matter was prepared. Each section of the kit carried a brief introduction describing how the panel manufacturer could use the sales tool in that section. A trial supply of each of the materials was imprinted with the customer's signature and presented to him by the company salesman after a showing of his copy of the moving picture. With the kit was included a price list for additional supplies "at cost."

No attempt has been made in the ten foregoing cases to convey the creative excellences the IA&SP discipline and its practitioners can build into the tools themselves. Marketing executives, whose interests and responsibilities are in fields other than copywriting and the graphic arts, may wonder what these barely described tools might look like when completed. And, indeed, there can be a wide span of quality in the creation of the advertisements, the printed matter, and the other promotion tools. However, management can rest assured that if the underlying principle of "what the tool is supposed to do" is clearly understood and adhered to, the finished product's effectiveness will invariably justify its cost.

Every step of IA&SP tool building requires expertise—from the adroit selection and use of media, to clear and concise copywriting, to clean and effective layout, to quality printing. Such expertise the IA&SP practitioners can bring to the task. What they cannot do, however, is lay the foundation for promotion. This is a task for marketing management and a critical one—it determines the role and the effectiveness of promotion in the marketing mix.

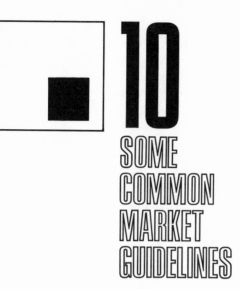

10
SOME COMMON MARKET GUIDELINES

Many American companies are expanding their marketing into the European Common Market. Observing some of the following guidelines may help promotion practitioners in their task of sales support for Continental marketing. Although the general approach to IA&SP planning as covered in the preceding chapters remains the same, the construction and use of the tools involve a variety of problems not encountered in the U.S. These are rooted in language, cultural mores, and methods of business operation.

A major step toward understanding and coping with these problems is to recognize the differences that exist in the business and industrial practices in European countries. We will take up some of the most fundamental.

In approaching the problem of promotional support for industrial products in the Common Market, it is first essential to disabuse oneself of the idea of "Europe." Europe is a conglomeration of nations. Companies that a U.S. manufacturer might regard as prospective "European" customers have little sense of identification with "Europe." Rather, they consider themselves "French," "German," "Dutch," "Italian," "Belgian," as the case may be. They rightfully draw back from—or at least look askance at—any media advertising, sales literature, or direct mail that ignores their ethnic separateness. This sense of cultural individuality is extremely strong. The separatism has been built up by centuries of custom, indigenous business practices, national pride, and personal fears. It has been ingrained by wars, tariff boundaries, and emotional attitudes. Cultural integrity is the basis for the individual charm of each nation; and it is the paramount fact of life that must be observed in doing business and creating promotion material. In producing advertisements and printed matter, it is essential for effectiveness, acceptance, and credibility to be as German, French, Italian, or whatever, as possible, but not "European."

To do this, promotion tools must be created or re-created on the spot by competent nationals familiar with the particular national market. The most common industrial marketing problems encountered by U.S. firms are the Phase 1 type. These most frequently require the basic tools of literature, salesmen's demonstration aids, direct mail, and media advertising. While a general promotion-program concept can be developed by U.S. thinking, the tools suitable for American use cannot simply be directly translated into several national languages and have maximum effectiveness, for the following reasons:

1. The benefits that are considered paramount in the American industrial nexus may not be benefits in a particular European country. The classic example in the consumer home appliance field is the U.S. manufacturer who advertised his dishwashers in Germany, trumpeting the work burden the machine removed from the housewife. Sales were nil. However, when the dishwasher was advertised as making the dishes cleaner because it used water too hot for human hands the sales were satisfactory indeed. With industrial products serving a highly developed, highly competitive, and largely automated U.S. industry, altogether different use benefits may prevail in the various European countries.

2. English words rarely have identical meanings and their connotations will be altogether different in each of the various European languages. In promotion material used in the United States, the word "new" automatically connotes "improved." In German and French, the word for "new" connotes "untried" and may even suggest substitution. Similarly, the term "cost-saving" in American-English parlance connotes something desirable; in German, this same term strongly suggests cutting corners and deterioration of quality. And practitioners might note that there are numerous instances in German industries where the lowest cost material is rejected because "quality" maintenance

is paramount. In consequence, the words used as well as the benefit appeals have to be adjusted to the national attitudes.

3. Supporting technical data is different in each country. The measurement of "horsepower" is radically different in various countries, and beyond that, there are differences in ready comprehensibility of units for reporting such values as gallons per minute, viscosity of liquids, burst strengths of film and paper, adhesive power, and the hundreds of others that describe the characteristics of materials or the performance of equipment. An engineer accustomed to comprehending "kilograms per square centimeter" cannot readily get the same understanding from "pounds per square inch." And it is to the seller's advantage not to make this conversion necessary. Aside from the differences in units, there are the differences in testing methods. While American Society Test Methods are widely used, ASTM values—even expressed in the metric system—are not universally used. In England, the British Standards methods are well entrenched; in Germany, the Deutsch Industrie Normen methods. Because of differences in methods, values of the different systems are not recalculable for direct conversion. Further, in most U.S. industries there are well-established "industry tests" such as the Cobb Test and ink flotation test used in the paper industry and the Shell Four-Ball Wear Test used in the automotive and petroleum industries. Some have crossed international boundaries. But many of these common, accepted "industry" evaluations are assessed by different methods in other countries. Some U.S. industry tests may be completely unknown and therefore the values they report meaningless. And of course, there is the bane of all tabular material, or indeed the reporting of all figures—the fact that Continentals use a decimal point for separating series digits and a comma for a decimal point. Thus, in American advertising, a tank that held 7,050.5 gallons would be a big tank. Reported in that way on the Continent, it would be a tank you could carry under your arm. To make it seem as big as it is, it would have to be said to contain 7.050,5 gallons—but far, far better would be to show it containing 26.686,1 liters. The British do not interchange the American separating marks, but of course there is a marked difference in quantity between the British and American gallon, bushel, and ton. A Swedish mile is approximately 10 kilometers.

The following practical guidelines should aid the practitioner in dealing with such problems.

1. Check program concepts with a *knowledgeable* local practitioner or advertising agency versed in the special industrial field.

2. Re-create all promotion tools with local practitioners in the national market to find the most appropriate selling appeals.
3. Do not attempt direct translations of U.S. promotion materials at a far remove (such as New York or London), particularly if they are to be used in several countries.

The formula for re-creating technical advertisements and literature is shown below.

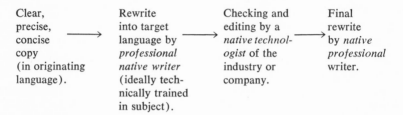

| Clear, precise, concise copy (in originating language). | → | Rewrite into target language by *professional native writer* (ideally technically trained in subject). | → | Checking and editing by a *native technologist* of the industry or company. | → | Final rewrite by *native professional* writer. |

The professional ability of the rewriter must at least equal that of the originator. Because a man is German, it does not necessarily mean he is a German writer; because he is an expert in a particular technology, it does not necessarily mean he is a writer *at all*. While professional writing competence is readily obtainable, it is not easy to find it joined to a thorough knowledge of a specialized field and its technical terms. A professional French writer, though thoroughly familiar with the English language, will be baffled by such terms as "limit torque," "bulk modulus," "dielectric strength," and "tensile elongation." Each language has its technical patois, and it cannot be translated literally. The industrial advertiser therefore must stick to the formula if he doesn't want his communication to be distorted or made to look ridiculous.

With promotional materials whose U.S. versions are to be adapted to foreign markets, loose, uncrowded layouts and an ample amount of "air" around illustrations are essential. One reason is that English is the most condensed language. Identical copy translated and typeset in French or German will require 15 to 20 percent more space. But more important, if the re-creation in the particular language is followed, the spacing required for copy and headlines will vary greatly, almost always requiring far more space for body copy. Tight layouts can be disastrous—a squandering of plate costs.

There are other essential differences that relate to advertising agencies and their service capabilities, media, and promotion practices. In the developed countries of Europe, multiagency use—even within a single country—is far more prevalent in industry than it is in the United States. Further, publications will accept advertising direct from clients, and media costs are negotiable. It is not unheard of, particularly in France, for an advertiser to have several agencies "bid" on carrying out a program, or to let pieces of a single program to two or more agencies. For more permanent agency relationships, it is not uncommon for the agency to seek a contract that stipulates a yearly level of promotion expenditure. Then, if this level is not reached, it bills for the difference.

Until quite recently, a given publication's circulation was more or less its trade secret. Within the last few years, however, circulation figures have been revealed increasingly and the practice of circulation audits has taken root. However, except in the case of a few relatively new industrial publications and some isolated well-established ones with progressive publishing policies, there is a dearth of audience information and reader profiles. There is also a sparsity of communication vehicles and a horrendous production-cost problem for media use.

In Germany, there is a prestigious and authoritative magazine entitled *Coal, Oil, Natural Gas, & Petrochemicals*. In the United States, this same editorial span is covered by not one, but—an estimate arrived at after some rough checking—14 publications. In virtually every European market, the industrial advertiser must accept a huge portion of waste circulation.

There is significant spillover that can be a bonus or a liability. German publications have a significant readership in Scandinavia, Holland, and the German cantons of Switzerland. French publications are read in southern Belgium, in the French cantons of Switzerland, and in Italy. Dutch-language technical publications that would be read in Holland and the Flemish north of Belgium are few and greatly generalized. Aside from the costs of special plates for language, the page sizes and mechanical requirements of Continental publications are still awaiting a first step toward practical standardization. Although mechanical costs in England and on the Continent are relatively much lower than in the United States, the ratio of advertising production costs to space costs for a trans-European program are shocking.

Certain facets of Continental promotion practices are to the advantage of the American practitioner. In using the media tool, he can shine by adhering to the creative standards set by effective industrial advertising—facts and demonstration. The majority of Continental industrial-publication advertising is far less sophisticated than its American counterpart. Much of it appears to have no other specific objective than to display the company's name and to itemize its products. By contrast, the industrial sales and technical literature is overwhelming in its detail, quality, and completeness.

Advertising inquiries from European publications present a special kind of problem, not to mention the letter inquiries that may reach the advertiser in as many as four different languages. Rarely will an inquirer reply to an advertisement's complete signature; most inquiry letters will simply be addressed to the company. If the company is a multi-department American firm and the inquiry letter must first be translated, there can be quite a delay. However, the inquirer is rarely a coupon clipper or a casual seeker of information. If the inquiry is not answered promptly, the advertiser can expect a follow-up letter that references the first inquiry to its subject—a letter and number code used only by that particular inquirer-company. It is much to the advantage of the advertiser to answer inquiries promptly and with full information.

It is a mistake to think that an inquiry from a good prospective company can be followed by a field representative. In most medium-size Continental firms, no matter who writes the letter, it is signed by the managing director. In large companies, it is signed by an upper management man who may have control of several departments. Thus the unintelligible reference "code" on the inquiry letter must appear on the addressed reply. This is the key that will get the printed literature through the company to the original letter writer. If international spill-over circulation and the broad span of technology covered mean waste circulation for the American industrial advertiser, the publication's intense readership virtually guarantees that the advertisement will be read. The Continental is not flooded with reading matter. He buys and reads. It was suggested earlier that it is far less essential in American industrial (as compared to consumer) advertising to "grab" the reader, that he reads industrial publications for information. This is even more evident on the Continent. It is not unusual to receive inquiries about an advertisement as long as two years after it has appeared.

The service of a local, "native" advertising agency is essential in each country in which marketing is to be carried out. The quantity of service provided by such agencies is incredible even for minuscle billings. In selecting a Continental agency, it is important for the American firm either to make direct contact with a suitable agency in each specific country or to work with a trans-European agency with wholly owned offices in each country where promotion is to be carried out. There are a number of trans-European agencies that operate primarily out of England and America that have "correspondent" agencies in various countries. In this system, the local correspondent carries out work for the account-holding agency on a split-fee basis. It is obvious that such split-fee work gets less input than wholly owned local accounts—particularly for industrial advertising, where the overall billing is low. However, a single, multinational agency (which by nature is a large operation) cannot on the average provide the intense service of local agencies (by nature, small) on low-billing industrial accounts.

Aside from the level of service, close attention to the promotion programs by a painstaking native agency is essential from a legal, as well as a value-received, standpoint. European industrial publications are downright venal. In many, a given amount of advertising space entitles you to a given amount of editorial attention. This is publicity, valuable and free. The interested native agency sees that you get it. In addition, there are legal observances to which an interested and committed local agency will be sensitive. For example, it is illegal and *verboten* in Germany to state categorically that any product is best, and it is also illegal to make comparisons with other products if the identity of those can be inferred. There, an American Motors statement, "More powerful than the largest selling one of the low-priced three," would constitute grounds for legal action by Chevrolet or Ford if either were the largest seller. Even comparisons with generic kinds of equipment or chemical compounds can create legal difficulties unless the comparison represents a contribution to basic technical knowledge or an advancement in technology. It is safe to give data on one's own product, but highly risky to make comparisons with another.

However, in the midst of differences, despite the pitfalls of language, varying cultural values, and unusual agency relations, and aside from the problems of accurate technical communication, frustrating media selection, and baffling inquiries, the principles of sound orientation that have been the subject of this book still apply. The differences are not in the principles involved in developing effective programs, but in the manner of their execution.

EPILOGUE

Six times in the preceding pages we have repeated in various ways that a thorough knowledge of the market is the sine qua non of crystallizing the sales problem, setting a specific, realistic marketing objective, and defining the pressure point upon which promotion can be brought to bear. This repetition has followed the old advertising aphorism: "You've got to tell 'em you're going to tell 'em, tell it, tell 'em what you've told 'em, then tell 'em again and again."

Three times we have repeated that the analysis of the sales problem is the sales or marketing planner's responsibility—that the pressure point he defines is the most essential ingredient in the creation of an industrial promotion program. It therefore follows that the effective and successful use of promotion by an industrial company is principally to the credit of the marketing planner or its sales management. And this is true. The promotion practitioner or the advertising agency or both can make the difference between "Promotion helped" and "Our promotion program was extremely successful." But to cross the borderline between "ineffective" and "effective," IA&SP is dependent on marketing direction, not on creative initiative or capability. It might be compared to a jeep, its engine idling, trailing a tow chain. Field salesmen are laboring to move a load of bricks along the road. Sales management can designate a point at which to attach the tow to the load, or it can have part of the bricks put into the jeep, or it can send the jeep for food and water. It can also choose to concentrate entirely on the load and the exertions of the laborers—while the jeep either stands idle or runs in meaningless circles around the job site.

The frequency and the degree of IA&SP use in the marketing mix is as much a mark of highly developed professionalism in marketing management as the effectiveness of the sales force or the astuteness of the marketing plan.

*There is no problem in industrial marketing
to whose solution IA&SP cannot contribute.*

INDEX

generic trade tasks, 38–43
German publications, advertising in, 127–133
goodwill advertising, 32–34
government relations advertising, 52

Hammond Company, in case study, 36–37
Harvard Business Review, 3
"how it works" element, in sales literature, 20–21

ideas, communication of, 14
impact value, in direct mail, 25
inappropriate design and layout, as "impotence" factor, 11, 17
Industrial Advertising and Sales Promotion (IA&SP)
    as "art of getting people to think and act," 87
    as communication, 13
    constant contact programs in, 45–47
    coordination in, 5
    "creative" vs. "administrative" personnel in, 73
    creativity in, 70–71
    discipline in, 87, 96
    "effective" vs. "ineffective" kinds of, 135
    field selling assists by, 43
    foundation for, 49–57
    frequency of use of, 136
    function of, 2
    genuine capability of, 6–7
    guidelines in creation of, 17
    "impotent" factors in, 8–12
    inappropriate design or layout in, 11, 17
    innovation obligation in, 5–7
    integrated programs in, 88
    jobs performed by, 35–47
    marketing objectives in, 55–56, 59–60
    marketing phases in, 39–40

market planning assistance from, 42–43
    monitoring obligation in, 7–12
    planning and packaging of, 4, 88–91
    positioning of in organization, 3
    program creation in, 67–75, 88–91
    program evaluation in, 92–94
    program launching in, 89–91
    program maintenance in, 91–92
    program pretesting in, 92
    responsibility function in, 5
    task promotion programs in, 44
    tools for, 7–8, 13–34, 90–91
industrial marketing
    vs. consumer, 57–58, 68
    as need-satisfying relationship, 69
    pressure point in, 56–65
industrial promotion, *see* Industrial Advertising and Sales Promotion (IA&SP); *see also* promotion; promotion programs
industrial relations advertising, 52
inferior quality, as "impotence" factor, 9
"influentials," identifying and reaching of, 17, 82
innovation, obligation of, 5–7
inquiries
    through advertising, 16
    from Continental customers, 132
international markets, 127–133

labels, as advertising, 36
Lancaster Process Controls Co., case study of, 113–116
Lanning, Irving, 74
Levitt, T., 3
literature, sales, *see* sales literature
Loft Packaging Products Co., case study of, 116–120

Manchester Paint Corp., case study of, 96–100
market
    anatomy of, 56, 59–60

market (*continued*)
expansion of, 84
knowledge of, 56, 135
market coverage, sales calls in, 81–82
marketing, vs. product selling, 53
marketing analysis, sales planning and, 53
marketing campaign, basic strategy of, 74
marketing management
market knowledge by, 56, 59
pressure point and objectives of, 56, 59, 60–63
three inputs of, 56, 59
marketing objectives, setting of, 60
marketing planning, IA&SP assistance in, 42–43
marketing progression, phases in, 39–40
marketing tasks, examples and case studies of, 95–125
markets, concentration on, 54–55
market segments, 54
Materials Handling, 61
McGraw-Hill Book Company, 46
media advertising, 15–18, 72–75
evaluation of, 93
repetition in, 79
time needed for, 85
models and parts exhibits, 26–27
Modern Hospital, 105
monitoring obligation
in IA&SP programs, 7–12
promotion tools and, 7–8, 13–34, 89–91
motion pictures, 123

need satisfaction, in industrial marketing, 69
Nestor Corp., case study of, 103–106
new product, three phases in marketing of, 39–40

opening "sell," in sales literature, 20–21

overdiffusion, as advertising and promotion error, 11–12

Packaging, 102
performance tests, physical exhibits and, 26
personnel, attracting of, 52
physical demonstration, items and exhibits in, 25–28
plant signs, as advertising, 36
point of no return, in advertising, 16
Power Gear and Control Company, case study of, 108–111
preferred-supplier position, 82–83
"preselling" advertising, 83
preselling function, 42
presentations, *see* sales presentations
pressure point, 60–65
case studies in, 62–63, 97–98, 101, 104, 106, 109, 111, 114, 117, 121, 123
creativity and, 71
defined, 55–56
promotional task at, 80
in promotion planning, 89–90
writing of, 89–90
pressure program, exploitation in, 72
pretesting, 92
price disadvantage, as "impotence" factor, 8
production cost, media appearances and, 15
product literature, 22–24
see also sales literature
product selling
vs. marketing, 53
steps in, 80–81
product selling programs, 53–57
budget for, 80
evaluation of, 93
program concept, in case studies, 98–99, 101, 109–110, 112–115, 118, 121, 123
program operation, in case studies, 100, 103, 108, 110–111, 113, 115–116, 120–122, 124–125

program tools, in case studies, 99–100, 105, 110, 113, 115, 118–119, 121–123

promotion
"float" syndrome in, 88
product selling and, 52–57
see also Industrial Advertising and Sales Promotion (IA&SP)

promotion programs
aptness in, 71
budgets for, 77–85, 90–91
consistency in, 71
cost of, 85
creation of, 67–75
creative capability in, 70–71
evaluation of, 79–80, 92–94
integration in, 88
launching of, 88–90
maintaining of, 91–92
pressure point in, 62–65, 89–90, 101–123
"selling proposition" in, 67
timing and coordination in, 72–73
tools in, 13–34, 90–91
see also Industrial Advertising and Sales Promotion (IA&SP); program concept; program tools

promotion tools, 7–8, 13–34, 90–91

prospects, finding of, 82

reminder advertising, 32–34
repetition, in media advertising, 79, 135
research and development, product improvement and, 54–55
rolling stock insignia, as advertising, 36

sales brochures, 99
see also sales literature
sales calls
time spent on, 83
value of, 81–82
sales conventions, attracting attendance to, 27–28

sales literature
cover title and illustration of, 19–20
educational or explanation function of, 22–24
objectives of, 18–19
selling elements in, 21
as tool in IA&SP, 18–22
salesman, increasing effectiveness of, 84
sales planning, marketing analysis and, 53
see also promotion programs
sales presentations
as sales tool, 29–32
tone and techniques in, 29–32, 99
sales problems, case studies of, 95–125
sales tools, 7–8, 13–34, 89–94
selling circuit, 53
"selling proposition," in promotion program, 67–69
slide presentations, 64
sound motion pictures, 123
stationery, as advertising, 36

task promotion programs, 44, 85
see also promotion programs
technical competence program, 51
technical data, in European advertising, 129
technical product literature, 22–24
technological change, IA&SP in, 9–10, 17, 42
Time, 118
time per call, reduction of, 83
timing and coordination, in promotion programs, 72–73
tools, promotion, 7–8, 13–34, 89–92
trade exhibits, 27
audiovisuals and, 29
photographs of, 72
trademarks, creation of, 36–38
"traditionitis," as "impotence" factor, 10–11